THE BOOK OF BERRYNARBOR

Stella,

Ron Toms

To my 'star'!
lots of love &
best wishes —
   Judith x.

Hope you enjoy the read.

THE BOOK OF
BERRYNARBOR

A Biography of Devon Life from 1920

JUDITH ADAM

With illustrations by James Young

HALSGROVE

> DEDICATION
> *For my father, a 20s child, who gave me my fascination and interest in the English language.*

First published in Great Britain in 2012

Copyright © Judith Adam 2012

All rights reserved. No part of this publication may be reproduced, stored in a retrieval system, or transmitted in any form or by any means without the prior permission of the copyright holder.

British Library Cataloguing-in-Publication Data
A CIP record for this title is available from the British Library

ISBN 978 0 85704 187 6

HALSGROVE
Halsgrove House,
Ryelands Business Park,
Bagley Road, Wellington, Somerset TA21 9PZ
Tel: 01823 653777   Fax: 01823 216796
email: sales@halsgrove.com

Part of the Halsgrove group of companies.
Information on all Halsgrove titles is available at: www.halsgrove.com

Printed and bound in the UK by T J International Ltd

Contents

Acknowledgements 4

Berrynarbor: A Nineteenth and Early Twentieth Century Description 5

The First View of this Village 7

Author's Note 8

Map: North Devon Parishes 10

Chapter One   Early Years and First Home 11

Chapter Two   Schooldays and Childhood Christmases 25

Chapter Three   'Henton Hill', the Village and Nearby 46

Chapter Four   First Employment and Life in the '30s 74

Chapter Five   Farming Life 82

Chapter Six   Animal Actions 117

Chapter Seven   Time Out 122

Chapter Eight   Second World War and Married Life 130

Appendices 146

Bibliography 155

Subscribers 157

Acknowledgements

Many people deserve thanks, but first and foremost, these should be given to Mike Patterson, who started me on this trail. A friend of Ron's, he told me that he had a story to tell.

I would like to thank Ron for allowing this newcomer to the village to ask him numerous questions, on an almost-weekly basis, about his family and working life. As those that know him, once he starts talking about something, he proves he is a mine of information. Thank you, for a fascinating insight into this beautiful part of the world and what life was like, 'in (your) young day.' It has been a pleasure to get to know you. Thank you too for your patience; this 'project' began as typed notes, and over a period of time, a book has evolved. His old photographs and those from his daughter, Sheila, are featured.

Many others have contributed, not least my 'long-suffering' husband! Every loaned image has been photographed by him, so that people, places and things could become the visuals needed to illustrate Ron's many topics. With a lifetime career in journalism, public relations and marketing, this knowledge has helped to guide this book towards completion.

Thankfully, Ron's school still survives and thrives. Staff and ex-staff of Berrynarbor Primary School, Headteacher Sue Carey, Mary-Jane Newell and Barbara Jordan have all given their time and valued information. The discovery and use of two historical School Registers, found during my research for this book, has contributed greatly.

Based at Barnstaple's Library, North Devon Records Office staff, have been patient and willing to provide enlightening and accurate additions or clarifications. This town's Museum is one of four that have supplied delightful photographs and postcards, generously; managers and volunteers from Braunton, Combe Martin and Ilfracombe have also loaned and informed.

Other organisations have also loaned images and given information: Haydon Edwards, a previous owner of Hele Mill, volunteers of the West Country Historical Omnibus and Transport Trust (WHOTT) and Antonie Haines: a family member and current owner of Watermouth Family Theme Park and Castle.

Local contributors have been many: Wendy Applegate, Nick Barten, Tom Bartlett, Mr and Mrs Boyer, Phil and Chris Brown, the current owners of 'Middle Lee': Ron's first home, Tim and Jill Massey, Dave Richards of Moules Farm, Bett Richards and Michael Richards, Jill Sidebottom, a grand-daughter of Fred Richards, Ron's 'Boss, and Gary Songhurst. I would like to extend thanks to Tom Bartlett, who has loaned and dated views from his substantial postcard collection and a particular thank you to Lorna Bowden who was able and willing to lend me so many personal photographs and postcards from her family's past.

Thanks must also be given to the illustrator and my 'editing team'. These book illustrations are the first done by James Young BA Hons. I am grateful, truly, for his willingness to change any aspect of any drawing; I know that he has spent many hours researching, observing and producing.

Finally, general editing help has been provided by Jill Massey, and the agricultural pages were checked and read by Bernard Newton, a one-time colleague and long-standing friend of Ron's.

J.D.A.

Berrynarbor: A Nineteenth and Early Twentieth Century Description

Extracts from some 19th- and early 20th-century issues of William White's *Devonshire Directories* and *Kelly's Directories* provide the following descriptions relating to the village and parish of Berrynarbor as it was.

'**BERRYNARBOR** is a pleasant village, on an eminence near the sea coast, overlooking Combemartin Cove, 3 miles E. of Ilfracombe. Its parish contains 899 inhabitants, and 4958A.1R.27P [acres, rods and perches] of land, including many scattered farm-houses, &c., and a range of hills in which lime and other stone is got. Westcote[1] says it was originally called Bury, and afterwards *Bury Nerbert*, from the family who held it some centuries ago, but we find it was held by the Berry family till 1708. A.D. Bassett, Esq., who has a pleasant seat here, called *Watermouth*, owns a great part of the parish, and is lord of the manor, which was purchased by J.D. Bassett, Esq., in 1712. Sir P.B. Chichester, Sir P.F. Palmer Acland and the Executors of the late Charles Cutcliffe, have estates here. Mr Bassett is also lord of the manors of *East Haggington* and *Woolscott*. The parish has its annual feast or revel on the first Sunday in July, and was the birthplace of the celebrated Bishop Jewel.[2] The *Church* is an ancient structure, with some monuments of the Berry Family. The *Church House*[3] was given by *John Berry*, in 1697, for the residence of poor parishioners.' **(1850)**

St Peter's Berrynarbor. Lych Gate and Church House, early 19th century. (House was in existence in 1831).

'... is a parish and village, in the Northern division of the county, South Molton hundred, Barnstaple union and county court district, rural deanery of Sherwell, archdeaconry of Barnstaple and diocese of Exeter... The roads in this parish are rugged and the farmhouses much scattered. Near the church is the old manor-house, now converted into a farmhouse. The chief crops are oats and barley; a great portion of the land is pasture... and the population in 1861 was 775.' **(1866)**

'... (has) a very handsome parsonage, in the Gothic style... built in 1862 by the present rector. Rev. Arthur

---

1 Thomas Westcote: the Devon historian born in 1567.
2 Bishop John Jewell, (1522-1572) became Bishop of Salisbury and was a Protestant Reformer and, apparently, Queen Elizabeth I's favourite bishop. Once documented as 'Buden', his home is shown as Bowden Farm on current O.S. maps.
3 The drawing shows that this 'House' was situated to the right of the church steps and would have faced 'Dunchideock'. It was found in Combe Martin church.

Crawfurth Bassett, J.P. is lord of the manor. The population in 1871 was 751.' **(1873)**

'The church ...consists of chancel, nave, south aisle and tower containing 6 bells... the stained east window erected in 1861 is a memorial to Samuel Thomas Slade Gully and W. A. Slade Gully M.A; there is also a stained window erected in the south aisle in 1883 to the memory of Miss Basset, of Watermouth Castle (and) in the vestry is an engraved portrait of Bishop Jewel, presented to the church by the Rev. Aubrey Townsend B.D. in 1861 [removed in the 80s]. There are sittings for 300. The living (includes) 125½ acres of glebe. The population in 1881 was 683.' **(1883)**

'... is 3 miles east of Ilfracombe Railway Station... is in Braunton petty sessional division (and) Braunton hundred. The Manor House stands near the church (and) is now in a dilapidated condition. The Independents have recently erected a new Chapel here. The National School... was recently enlarged and improved at an expense of £100.' **(1890)**

'The manor house stands near the church; part of the front, including the porch, was taken down in 1889, and the porch has been re-erected at Westaway,[4] near Barnstaple; the exterior was formerly ornamented with shields of arms of the Plantagenet, Bonville and other families, and elaborate carved work, all of which has been removed to Watermouth Castle, the seat of Mrs Basset, lady of the manor and principal landowner. The handsome parsonage... was erected in 1860 at a cost of more than £2000. The population in 1891 was 652. The National School (mixed) erected in 1847, to hold 150 children; average attendance, 90'. **(1893)**

'...the lych gate on the south side of the churchyard was erected in 1671'. 'The population in 1901 was 589.' **(1902)**

'...the Village Hall and Club House, erected in 1908, was the gift of Mrs Basset. The Manor Hall, erected by Mrs Penn-Curzon in 1913, is used for concerts, meetings &c. The population rose in 1911 to 594.' **(1919)**

'Watermouth Castle, now unoccupied, is an embattled mansion of stone, erected about 1825 ...Mrs Penn Curzon is the principal landowner. The population in 1911 was 594.' **(1923)**

'...in the churchyard is a cross erected in memory of the men of the parish who fell in the Great War, 1914-18. Watermouth Castle (is) the residence of Mrs. Penn Curzon C.B.E... (and) the population in 1921 was 534.' **(1930)**

In **1939**, Kelly's stated the village was 'in the Barnstaple division of the county... in the rural deanery of Shirwell. The living is a rectory (with) 18 acres of glebe. The population in 1931 was 561.'

These extracts are almost the equivalent of Ron's lifetime; they span a period of Berrynarbor's history of almost 90 years. They are documented reminders that nothing stays the same: people, places and things have all altered in some way. By '1919', the 'population' included our 'protagonist'.

---

4 'Westaway' was one of the Basset estates. The property still exists.

The First View of this Village

Berrynarbor about 1892. Reproduced from a F. Frith & Co Postcard

This is the oldest and clearest view found of the central village. In the left-hand corner, climbing above a ploughed field is Henton Hill, Henton Row or Haggington Row as it has been known and recorded. Now, the road sign shows it is 'Haggington Hill', but the ploughed field has gone. Silver Street, in the foreground, is the only other visible road.

The old Manor House was in its original state; **Kelly's Directory** *of 1866 stated that this has now been 'converted into a farmhouse.' Bessemer Thatch (centre left) stands to the left of the church steps. The school is located in Silver Street, on the left, its bell suspended above its roof. The church is without its weather vane.*

Author's Note

'History' has always been a fascination for me, so when a neighbour mentioned that there was a man of over ninety who had lived in Berrynarbor all his life, my curiosity was aroused. He was concerned that, if somebody didn't write this nonagenarian's story down on paper, his memories, about the village that he knew, would disappear when he died. I believed that a chance to glean information about this Domesday village and what 'life' had bestowed upon the young Ron and *his* neighbours was an unmissable opportunity and should be captured, permanently.

Ron Toms

Fortunately and coincidentally, many months later, as part of a school project, seven, eight and nine year-olds attending Berrynarbor Primary School were guided by their Head Teacher to create questions for Ron about his life, under the headings of: 'Travel and Transport', 'Memories of Childhood', 'Buildings and Homes', 'Adults', 'Boyhood and Adulthood' and 'How is School Different?'

I listened to these 21st-century schoolchildren asking their questions and was startled to realise that Ron's lifestyle had been *so* different from theirs *and* mine. His answers were an auditory history lesson and reference book.

It could be said that 'his village' is one of a dying breed, as it has all facilities: a church, school, shop, post office, two pubs and a village hall. Some have existed for centuries and contribute greatly to the success of this friendly, thriving, picture-postcard village, sited in an area of outstanding natural beauty, (AONB). Berrynarbor has also been a frequent 'Best Kept Village' award winner, including in 2010.

It is surrounded by farmland, but some farmhouses have become homes and their outbuildings have become holiday accommodation. Local produce is still available; villagers and tourists can enjoy fresh, unadulterated local produce here, but it is not as varied or as plentiful as it was in Ron's youth and working life.

For a man such as Ron, born during the first quarter of the twentieth century, changes since *his* birth have been countless and, perhaps, difficult to recall and appreciate. Domestic, scholastic, social and commercial developments must seem extraordinary for Ron and others of his generation, when they reflect. His reminiscences remind us just *how much* life has altered.

Most of Ron's education was gained by sitting at 'double desks with lift-up lids', but today's schoolchildren *expect* to gain knowledge inside and outside the classroom. In addition to textbooks, 'History' for them can be the castle or a museum visited on a school trip, television films or documentaries, school projects, a family's sepia or black and white photo-

AUTHOR'S NOTE

'Berry in Bloom' Best Kept Village.

graphs and personal experiences related by the older generation.

Apart from approximately two years, all of his working life was spent as a farm labourer. His unique memories are a valuable record, particularly of the numerous agricultural developments and of life in a rural community.

This is a personal portrayal of a Devonian life from the 1920s onwards, but there would be similarities all over the country. Wherever appropriate, 21st-century comparisons have been juxtaposed.

Throughout the main body text of this book the author's commentary appears in italics, with Ron's memories recorded in roman text within single quote marks.

J.D.A.

The Parishes of North Devon
(not to scale)

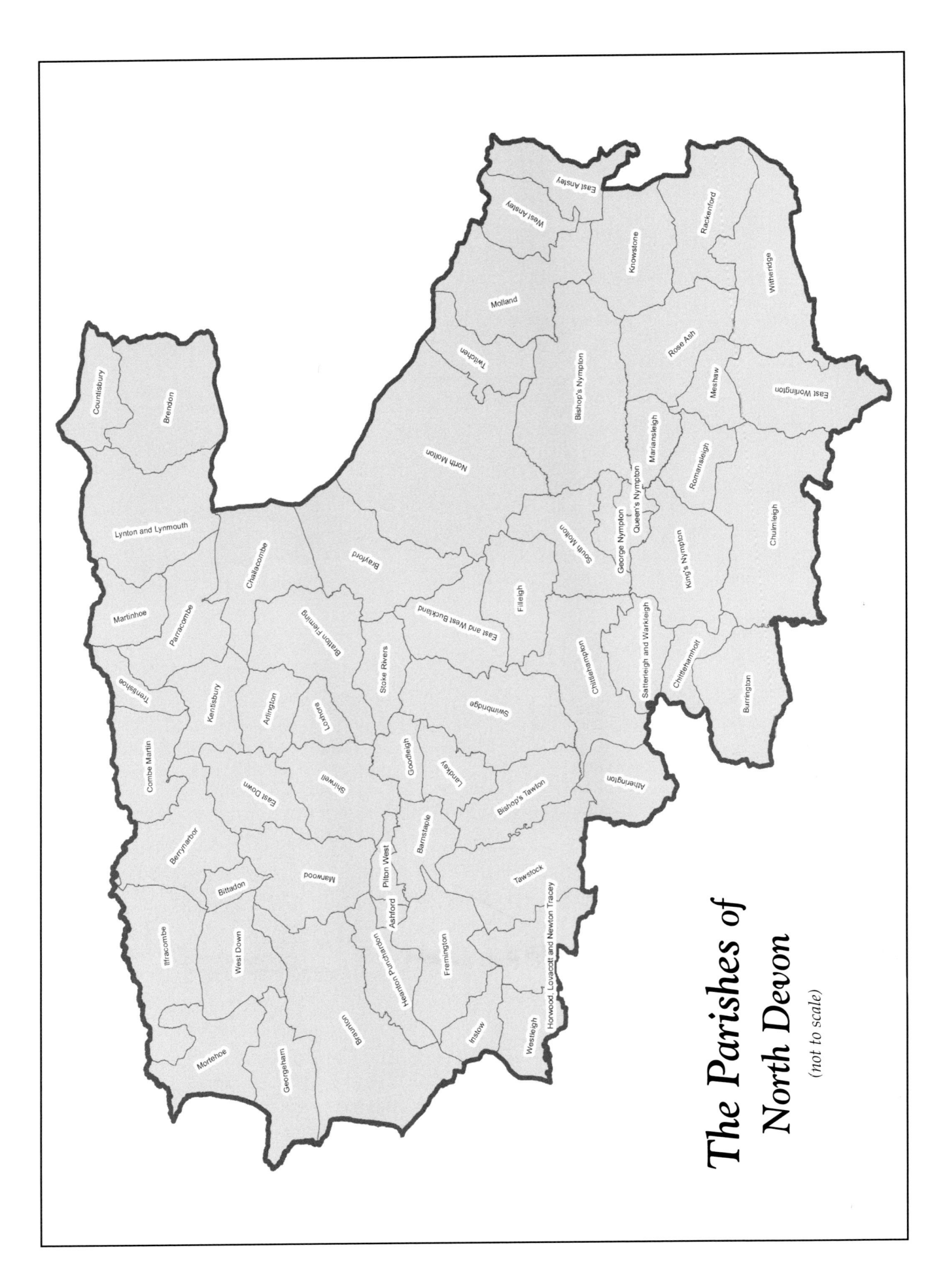

Chapter 1

Early Years and First Home

Ronald Francis Toms *was a First World War baby, born in the summer of 1916, on the 15th July, at home – Middle Lee Farm – in this 'pleasant village' that lies between Ilfracombe and Combe Martin in North Devon.*

If we put his birth date into context, King George V was on the throne with David Lloyd George as his Prime Minister; the novelist and poet Thomas Hardy was still very much alive, as was another 'Great Britain', the composer, Sir Edward Elgar. Regrettably, the Battle of the Somme had begun on the 1st July and raged for Ron's first five months, but, Howard Carter's discovery of Tutankhamun's tomb was still six years away. Closer to home, Wembley, synonymous with football, had not hosted its first cup final; 'The White Horse Cup Final' occurred on 30th April 1923, a few months before his seventh birthday.

As a four-year-old, Ron would have been unaware that his village was about to undergo what could be described as the beginnings of major 'change'. White's Devonshire Directory states that the 'Bassett' (sic) family had owned Watermouth and 'a great part of the parish' since 1712. Ron's first home was part of this estate, one of many tenanted properties. It is, perhaps, easy to forget that this was customary then: landed gentry owned their mansions, farms and cottages used by their workforce and, usually, large tracts of land.

Middle Lee Farm. Ron with his cousin, Reggie.
'I think I was about 11. Reggie was a little bit older than me, about 12.'

THE BOOK OF BERRYNARBOR

Watermouth Castle & Bay, c.1890.   Reproduced from a F. Frith & Co Postcard.

Watermouth Castle and Park.   A.J.V.I. Series

◇ EARLY YEARS AND FIRST HOME ◇

Watermouth Castle, Ilfracombe, c.1907.   E.T.W. Dennis

Watermouth Harbour.   Garratt, Bristol

On a summer's day in 1920, Middle Lee and a future home on Haggington Hill were two of more than forty properties auctioned. At the time, it was common for villagers to have such 'garden accessories' as a 'piggery', 'potato house' or a 'pump house'. These sale documents and Ron's descriptions enable us to compare the past and the present and remind us how time has transformed everything.

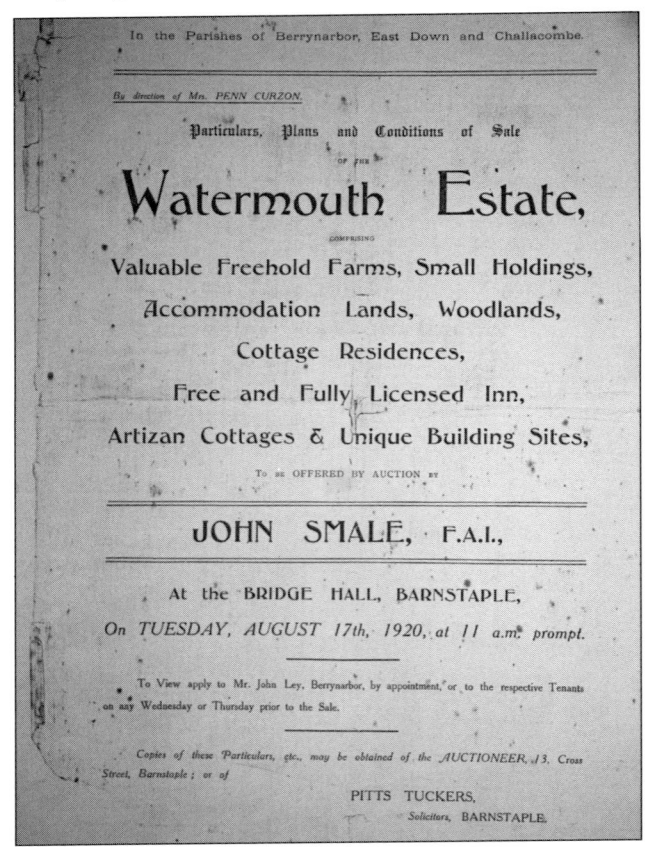

Particulars, Plans and Conditions of Sale of the Watermouth Estate.

For centuries, Middle Lee was a working farm. When Ron was a boy, it had 'big fields', because they were used for cattle and crops; 'no sheep were kept here, but they were on other farms.'

The original building stood in about 90 acres, which is small compared to some modern-day Devonian farms. White's refers to the village of 'Shirwell', which is ten miles from Berrynarbor. A farmer here farms 720 acres and has more than 370 milking cows; however, an East Down farm, approximately 5 miles from Ron's home, has 1800 acres, some of which is grazed by over 800 dairy cows.

Ron lived at Middle Lee, for seven and a half years, with his grandparents, Frank and Ellen Toms, who managed the farm, his Uncle Ernest and his mother, Hilda. The farmhouse had 'four down and three up'; bedrooms were often shared, but there was no bathroom.

In 1972 it was purchased to become a family home and conversions began on its outbuildings for holiday cottages; it is one of the many businesses in this locality that supports and participates in North Devon's tourist industry.

'Middle Lee was *small*, but I always wanted to work on a farm. The fields were *really* steep, so the corn was always cut by men with scythes. Three men, say, would cut it and behind them there could be another three. They'd follow each other. They'd have to be careful so as not to cut each other! It would be gathered up and tied in to six sheafs for one stack. The men would know how much to cut at any one time. There were always plenty of workers; *everyone* was willing to help.

We didn't have a lot of animals on the farm: cows, about half-a-dozen, and calves. They were mainly milking cows and we used to rear food to take to market.

There were no lorries then. If you had a freshly-calved cow, you'd keep the calf for a couple of weeks to make sure it was O.K. You'd put the calf in the cart, with the sides up, or a rope around its neck tied to the inside of the cart. The cow would follow, but somebody would follow her to make sure she didn't turn back, and you'd take both to market to sell.

You'd take it in turns. One of you would ride the horse and one would follow and you'd change for the journey home. It'd be me and Dan, my uncle; we'd go up the Haggington Hill and along Slew Lane. We'd keep off the main roads as much as possible, but there were no traffic lights and there wasn't much traffic then.'

Granny and Granfer: Mr Frank and Mrs Eilen Toms.

EARLY YEARS AND FIRST HOME

'In granny and granfer's time, on a Monday, we used to buy half-dozen or a dozen chickens from the Pannier Market [in Barnstaple][5] that were freshly killed. Granfer used to go in to the cattle market and me grandmother would go to the Pannier Market. Granfer was always known as Frank, but he could have been Francis.'

'Someone would drive the horse and cart and someone else would pluck the chickens on the way back from town: probably on that hill, Whitefield Hill, from Muddiford and Milltown [signed Berry Down and Combe Martin]. It's a long hill for a horse. We used to take them back to the market, plucked ready for baking, on a Wednesday or Thursday.

Barnstaple Pannier Market through the ages – 1855, 1938 and 1990s.

---

5   The Pannier Market has been in the town for over 150 years. It was completed in 1855 to ease congestion and protect buyers and sellers from the weather. Previously, they had lined the High Street, between Cross Street and lower Boutport Street, with their baskets or panniers.

Middle Lee: Mrs Toms' tea garden.

Middle Lee 2012.

'A horse would always know if he was going home; *he'd* be *off!* There were brakes on the market carts; going downhill, you'd have to be careful going round corners. When you got on the straight road you could let them go.

This was [drawing above] Middle Lee as it was when my granny had it. The tearoom was at the end. You could sit quite a few there when it was wet. The left hand-side building was part of the stable. It had a small, sloping roof over the pump house. The toilet shed was outside, across the road, on the left, under some trees and bushes and up two or three steps.

When I was really little, my grandparents were in one bedroom; her name was Pethrick before she married my grandfather. Ernest, her brother, had a room. I was in with me mother.

My uncle used to be in bed most of the time; he never married and he didn't mix. They used to take him his meals in bed. He would always come down for Sunday meals though.

At the back of the bedrooms, there was a separate set of wooden steps to the loft. It wasn't in the roof. We'd put all the 'rubbish' here. Well, not rubbish exactly, stuff we didn't need, but didn't want to throw away.

Downstairs there was a dairy, a kitchen where all meals were taken and the sitting room, known as the parlour, which was only used on high days and holidays. We lit the fire in the parlour for the first cup of tea. We put the kettle into the grate and put it amongst the sticks: the kindling. The fire would be going and we always had smoky tea for our first one!

There was a back kitchen; we didn't have any fancy names in them days! We washed the clothes here. Me mother used to take in washing and we washed ourselves here too. We had a lean-over-the-sink wash, but we bathed in front of the fire, in one of those long metal baths.

Dan and his wife Lizzie and my cousins, Reggie and Violet, lived in the Sterridge Valley [sometimes spelt 'Sterrage'], but after grandfer died, Dan, his son, took over. Farms are usually passed to sons. They moved into Middle Lee to take over the farm and for a while, there was my grandmother, Dan, Lizzie, my cousins, my uncle, my mother and me.

Entrance to Sterridge Valley
E.A. Sweetman & Son. Ltd., Tunbridge Wells

In my school days, Dan, Lizzie and my cousins left the farm and moved to Dormer House: Muffet's Tearoom.[6] They left because of Dan's ill health and they ran it as a bed and breakfast accommodation only. When Violet married Dave Goodman, they did bed and breakfast, the teashop and evening meals.

When they left the farm it was sold. It went out of the family. It may have been to Parky Smith. I know he farmed it.'

---

6 Current owners say that parts of the building date back to the 15th century.

◈ EARLY YEARS AND FIRST HOME ◈

Sterridge Valley, 1911.   Reproduced from a F. Frith & Co Postcard

Sterridge Valley, Berrynarbor.   Harvey Barton, Bristol

THE BOOK OF BERRYNARBOR

Berrynarbor looking West, 1920.   Garratt, Bristol
The building facing the road was 'Muffet's Tearoom', until 2011.

Berrynarbor looking West, 2012.

EARLY YEARS AND FIRST HOME

Middle Lee and Victorian Visitors.
'The lady outside the door looks like me mother and me grandfer is next to her.'

Bowden's Southlea Farm Berrynarbor.   E. Osborne & Co. Ilfracombe

Outside, the farmhouse has 'changed a bit'. It had a lean-to, which was roadside, where holidaymakers ate cream teas when it was wet. It is now part of the farmhouse.

Holidaymakers have been visiting this area and eating Devon cream teas since Victorian times; farmers have been able, and continue, to substitute their agricultural income with farm holidays.

'It was nothing fancy mind. It had a galvanised tin roof and a wall about three feet high [90 cms], there was no glass filling the gap, but people, the holidaymakers, were quite happy to sit there and have their tea. There was a small lawn opposite the side of the house and people sat there too when it was dry. It was noted for its cream teas. South Lee did them too.

Coaches with two horses used to come from Ilfracombe. You'd know, if the weather was good, they'd come. [7] When they used four horses to go to Lynton they even brought a double-decker coach with four horses [through the village]: *that* took about *eight* people! When they went to Lynton, they'd change their horses at the end of Combe Martin.'

The Capstone. Dearden & Wade Bournemouth
The Victorian Pavilion was converted into the Pavilion Theatre; this was completed in 1925. Several steamers made 'regular daily sailings' during the season, to Ilfracombe.

'There were two [ways to the village]: they'd use Smythen Hill and return over Haggington or they'd come over Haggington and return over Smythen. They'd have to use wheel drugs [drags] for the

Wildersmouth Beach and The Tors. The 'Imperial Hotel', foreground, stood where the Landmark Theatre stands now.

---

7 It is documented in 1936, that 'Ilfracombe had a record August Bank Holiday. It is estimated that there was an influx of 40,000 visitors.'

20

EARLY YEARS AND FIRST HOME

Ilfracombe from Capstone.

Wildersmouth Beach.   Photochrom Tunbridge Wells, Kent
A postcard posted in July 1955, the beach's popularity is obvious. The 'Pavilion' and bandstand are in the centre background.

Coach and four.[8] *Posters show that journeys included Lynton and Exeter. Bert Gear, the guard, stands with the horn, behind him is Mr Sam Colwill. The coach driver is Tom Colwill, his son.*

Sam Colwill's Office, Ilfracombe, July 1925. These premises would have been familiar to Ron, his family and friends.

---

8 'The coach and four' ran until 1910. Motorised vehicles, or charabancs, took over, but they still departed from the office of Sam Colwill Coach Proprietor, 96 The High Street, next door to the Queen's Hotel. This businessman was once Ilfracombe's Town Mayor. He was not its only coach proprietor; he had competition: Tom Copp had coach trips from the town, then charabancs for the holiday visitors as well.

EARLY YEARS AND FIRST HOME

A charabanc outing, 4 August 1923. T.I.C.
In the front row are: Percy Thorne, Ernest Richards and an unknown face. Second row: Jack Chubb, Alf Brooks and Alf Leworthy. Middle row: Sam Harding: Berrynarbor's blacksmith, Tom Leworthy: Alf's brother, and Dick Huxtable with grandson: Jack Snell. Fourth row: another couple of unknown faces and Will Sloley. Back row: Jack Draper, Dick Richards and Albert Jones.

coaches when they were going downhill.[9] Some of the passengers were nervous, so they'd walk up *and* down the hills. Sometimes they'd all be asked to walk!

I'd walk from Middle Lee over to the bottom of Smythen Hill to take a drug from off the wheel and I'd get a shilling [1/- or 5p]. The drug would be hanging on a chain underneath the coach. It was strong metal, but it was smart and tidy and you'd hang it back on.

Mrs Richards used to bring lavender to sell. When people came for tea, me grandmother couldn't see them, so they'd ring a bell and this is the one they'd ring [see opposite].'

Dick Hancock, who lived with his brother Jim, in 'Lower Town',[10] used to come every Sunday. Weather permitting, he used to walk to Middle Lee to buy a quarter of a pound of cream, [4ozs or 113grammes].

It would be in a cup or something like that. He'd pay six old pennies for it [2½ p] and just eat it. He'd walk around the house or the garden just chatting and eating it.'

The brass bell used to summon Ron's grandmother.

---

9   A braking or retarding device for the wheel of a horse-drawn vehicle.
10 'Lower Town' is known as 'Silver Street' today. It begins opposite the church and continues to the signpost at 'Turn Round'.

Part Of 'Lower Town'. E.A. Sweetman & Son. Ltd., Tunbridge Wells
An empty 'Lower Town' pictured in the 1930s, with the gable end of the school roof visible in the top left-hand corner. Bessemer Thatch, in the background to the right of this gable, retains its thatch, which means that this photo was taken before the fire that destroyed it on 5 May 1937. The village post office, now Briar Cottage, is the property on the right-hand side of this view.

Lower Town, 2012.

Chapter 2

Schooldays and Childhood Christmases

For many, perhaps all, junior schools nationwide, a school photograph is an annual event, but this is not just a 20th century innovation, as Ron can prove. This sepia image shows three members of staff and more than eighty schoolchildren gathered near Berrynarbor School. They posed in 1898, but Ron remembers three of them well.

Later photographs include Ron, his teachers and school friends, those that lived in the village and others that lived in nearby Berry Down. All illustrate aspects of change.

'*We* didn't wear uniforms to school but we had a bag with B.S. on it'. *In the photo below, clearly all the girls wore their white pinafores over their dresses and the boys donned caps, jackets and long shorts which gave them uniformity, but a 'varied wardrobe' for many working families, would have been unlikely.*

'I knew two of these boys as men. I knew Mr Brown, the Headmaster too; he lived at Fuchsia Cottage.'

Berrynarbor School photograph, 1898. At the front, on the ground, '3rd from the left, is James Ley.[11] He lived at Hole Farm. Standing, 2nd row, away from the wall, is Bruce Pedrick[12] or Pethrick. He's the third one along... to the teacher's left. He lived in the last house before Grattons... on Haggington Hill. James's son, Reg, [Reginald] married Bruce Pedrick's daughter.'

---

11 There is only one 'James Ley' recorded in the School Registers. His birth date is entered as 'Feb 18th 1891', so he was 7 years here. He is one of many men listed on the 'Roll of Honour', displayed in St Peter's Church, as serving with the 'North Devon Hussars' in September 1914. Frostbite forced his return from the First World War; he continued to live at Hole Farm, which he worked from 1918 with Eva Stanbury, his wife.

12 'Bruce Pedrick' is recorded with a birth date of '12.2.1888', so he would have been ten at the time of this photograph.

In 1920, four-year-old Ron and most of his classmates walked to what was originally built as a 'National School'[13] and, like all other children of his generation, he stayed at his village school for ten years only.

Admission seems to have been possible throughout the year, as two 'Admission Registers', have been discovered on school premises. Their entries begin on '1874 January 12th' and under 'DATE OF ADMISSION' every month appears.

One reveals that Ron started on the '6. 9. 1920' and his 'DATE OF LAST ATTENDANCE AT THIS SCHOOL' was '1.8.1930'. His 'REASON FOR LEAVING' was that he had reached '14 years of age'.

'I started in the summer, but summer holidays could be two weeks only. We didn't go away. We'd go to mates' farms and help with farming. I enjoyed it!'

It had been possible to start at Berrynarbor Infants' School from the beginning of the Spring Term, January, and the beginning of the Autumn Term, September; however, the school reverted to an annual intake as of September, 2011.

Today, children arrive at this school at four or five years of age but leave when they are eleven and, unlike Ron, progress to secondary school and further or higher education. Some will not cease formal education until their twenties.

Currently, the school register lists more than seventy names, and their first names include Josh, Roker and Morgan, Kelly, and Elyse, names unknown in Ron's day.

Ron was summoned to lessons at Berrynarbor Infants' School by a bell in the school tower. The tower is still there, but the bell is no longer. Today, for many years, one of the pupils, a random choice, is given the responsibility of ringing a hand bell in the playground just before 9.00 o'clock to call children to their classrooms.

School Register, 6th entry: 'Toms, Ronald Francis'

---

13 The National Society for Promoting Religious Education was a Church of England body in England and Wales, set up in 1811 to promote church schools. Historically, these were called 'National Schools', implemented by the local vicar and Church of England members. Pupils were taught arithmetic, reading, religion and writing.

SCHOOLDAYS AND CHILDHOOD CHRISTMASES

Village School, Silver Street façade, 2012.

When he left the infants' class, which was mixed, the genders were separated. Today, boys and girls, including those in the 'infants' class', known now as 'Reception and Year 1', sit side by side.

Ron's reminiscences about his teachers: i.e. that when the 'Misses' became 'Mrs' they left the profession, demonstrates how education has altered since his boyhood. It wasn't until The Education Act of 1944 that female teachers were allowed to retain their teaching positions after marriage. Speaking of his schoolmate Edward Courtney, [see photo on page 28] Ron recalled:

'Eddie was a little lad; 'e was a lill tacker.[14]

The head teacher, when I was there, was Miss Veale. She lived at Little Thatch, called Little Gables now. The window on the corner was a stable door. When she taught, it was the boys mainly, but she was there to help the other teachers if they needed her. Anything the teacher didn't understand, she'd put them right. She was *very* strict. When we arrived at school, you'd walk past her desk. She didn't have her own office, nothing like that. You had to stop and give your name for the register. She had her desk in the boys' room and the girls had to pass her to get to *theirs*. The little ones passed her too and they'd go through the girls' room to get to the Infants' room.

The other teachers were Miss Baulkwell; she taught the boys, and Miss Lily Richards; she became Mrs Huxtable. Lily Richards was my first teacher; she taught the infants. She lived at 36 The Village, then she married Fred Huxtable, a farmer's son at Woolscot, and they moved to Shirwell. Miss Muriel Richards replaced her. I don't think Miss Baulkwell married. I think the girls' teacher was Miss Rutter.

---

14 Ron's idiolect includes Devonshire dialect; a 'lill tacker' is a small boy.

Berrynarbor Infants School, 1920. Back row L to R: Verna Richards, Reginald Ley, Rachel Irwin, Vera Richards, Phyllis Watkins, Elizabeth Delbridge, and Miss Lily Richards. Middle row, L to R: Francis Huxtable, George Gear, Leslie Sydenham, Ronald Toms, Brenda Richards and George Irwin. Seated L to R: Charles Pinching, Albert Adams, Edward Courtney [with slate], Doris Cornish, Honor Irwin.

Berrynarbor Class 2 1920. Back row L to R: Teacher: Mabel Snell, Evelyn Ley, Doris Dinnicombe, unknown, Olive Street, Annie Seldon, Vera Latham, Ivy Nicholls. Middle row L to R: Ephraim Street, Ivy Hewitt, Lily Ley, Muriel Richards, unknown, Rhoda Challacombe. Seated L to R: Stanley Jones, unknown, Charlie Hockridge, Bill Irwin, ? Isaac, Lionel Dummett, Bert Irwin.

SCHOOLDAYS AND CHILDHOOD CHRISTMASES

From the road, the entrance was on the left of the school building, near the back. There were black metal railings with spikes outside the school. There was a dividing door between the boys' and girls' rooms and the infant room was at the back.

There were no electric lights when I first started school; we all had paraffin lamps. They were big lights, hanging from the ceiling. I think there were two in each room; we had to see what we were writing! They were looked after by a caretaker; he had to go up on a step ladder to light them with a match.

We always walked to school, even when I was little. There were few cars around then. Our school day was 9.00 'til 4.00, but if we misbehaved we stayed behind and wrote lines. Every morning we'd begin with a hymn. Every Friday morning, the Reverend Churchill would take our scripture lessons and prayers.

He'd arrive on his motorbike, probably because he was going on somewhere else: Ilfracombe probably. To get it going he'd have to push it and run alongside. When the engine started, he'd jump on!

If we were naughty, the parson would be called by the teacher. She'd send a pupil to go over to the Rectory to get him. It was usually for a boy, but he wouldn't make a great fuss or nothing, he'd just say, "Boys will be boys!"

We used to use slates and chalks in the very beginning. It was just a piece of slate, no frame. The teachers used a blackboard and an easel; we all used it. Then we used pens and ink.

The desks were wooden with inkwells and ridges for your pens that had nibs. The benches were fixed to the desk. They were flat and wooden with backs and there were two to a desk. We had homework at nights.

Our classroom walls were plain; no work went on the wall. We had a gramophone; it was an HMV. We had a dunce's cap and sat in the corner. Yes, I did wear it and I had the cane too!

Me mother was *always* at home, when I got home from school; she was *always* busy. When I came home, me granny used to say, "Do you want a slice of bread and butter?" She'd add jam and cream! The cream was real fresh cream, topped with a yellow crust. If I had a mate with me he'd be offered some too!'

'When I was a schoolboy, about nine or ten, we were told, during the school day, to go and help people. If it was frosty, icy or snowy, we'd go and help with their shopping. The teachers would know the old people in the village and we'd be pleased to help! Sometimes they'd offer a 1d or 2d, but we didn't do it for the money. The teacher could say

Miss Veale Headteacher (left), Miss Muriel Richards, (standing) and Miss Joan Wainwright. Possibly 1930s.

Children walking to school.

Berrynarbor School 1922 Classes I and II. Back row L to R: Arthur (Nip) Jones, Gladys Jones, Jim Huxtable, Doris Dummett, William Street, Phyllis Toms, Stanley Jones, unknown. 2nd row L to R: Miss Veale, Evelyn Ley, Doris Dinnicombe, Muriel Richards (b. 18.07.1911), Laura Ley, Alice Irwin, Beatty Huxtable, Lily Ley, Ivy Dinnicombe, Left, standing behind Lucy Gear is believed to be Muriel Yeo. 3rd row L to R: Lucy Gear, Ivy Watkins, Rhoda Challacombe, Olive Street, Annie Seldon, Myrtle Richards, Vera Latham, Gladys Seldon. Front row L to R: Reg Sydenham, Leonard Dummett, Lionel Dummett (holding the plaque), Ephraim Street.

someone isn't too good, so we'd look in and see if we could help. The school thought it was part of our education to help people in the village. We'd look in on people when we'd finished school for the day too. It wasn't just me; we were all willing to do it.'

Local children still walk to school, but pupils are no longer only 'from the village' and 'Berry Down'. They travel from outlying farms and villages such as Combe Martin, Parracombe and Woolacombe and the nearby town of Ilfracombe.

Staff numbers have increased; the majority of its fourteen staff are the teaching professionals: the head teacher, teachers and teaching assistants. They are supported by an administrator, caterer, a caretaker and peripatetic teachers of academia, music and sport.

The building he knew had three classrooms under one roof and one entrance, but like its pupils, the school and the playground have 'grown'. Additionally, there is a large, covered, open-air classroom, used for almost the entire academic year.

Facilities include boys' and girls' toilets and a kitchen and, an extension opened in 2006, means that there is now a library that functions also as an additional classroom, or meeting room when necessary, a staff room and two offices.

For twenty-five years, the 'little ones', Reception and Year 1, had the 'Parish Rooms',[15] which is one classroom, to themselves, but Year 5 and 6 (10 and 11-year olds) have taken up 'residence' here since September 2010.

'We learnt Sums, Scripture, Geography, History

---

15 *Kelly's Directory* (1919) comments that 'the Village Hall and Club House, erected in 1908, was the gift of Mrs Basset.' In living memory, it has always been known as the 'Parish Rooms'. In the past it was used by Bible Study Groups, Church Youth Clubs, and The Royal British Legion. It has been used by the school as an additional classroom for some 25 years.

SCHOOLDAYS AND CHILDHOOD CHRISTMASES

The Parish Rooms, 2012.

and English and my favourite was Sums: Mental Arithmetic. We had to count in our heads, no calculators then!

We used to go out for nature walks too and the teacher used to explain what things were. We used to pick the wild flowers and press them in a book in the school. There seemed to be quite a lot of wild flowers in them days, but they didn't use chemicals then... We didn't go anywhere else, no school trips then!

We had a music teacher who came in on Friday afternoons: Miss Earl. Those that didn't want to learn, they had to stay in school, but you could get a book and sit and read. It was a more relaxed afternoon. She lodged with me mother. She did music lessons private in the evenings.'

The primary curriculum has increased considerably since Ron's education concluded. If he were a pupil at his old school now he would learn: English, Maths, Science, French, Music, PE, History, Geography, Information and Computer Technology (ICT), Art & Design, Design & Technology and Personal, Social and Health Education (PSHE). Their Gardening Club is for all ages led by some parents and has some curriculum use.

In addition to the game of football that Ron played, *today's pupils play hockey, tri-golf, do gymnastics and athletics and are taken for swimming lessons at Ilfracombe's pool. Their break-time games are played with or without equipment on the playground or the grass.*

Eating and heating have changed too. Today's pupils have a choice of a cooked meal, freshly made in the kitchen, or their packed lunch, but Ron and his friends could not have a hot mid-day meal and, in the winter months and cold, wet days, he and his friends could not luxuriate in warmed classrooms either, even though radiators had been invented in the mid-19th century. Their heating was functional, dual purpose but unable to cope with the demands.

'There was no cookhouse; you couldn't have school dinners. People brought their sandwiches, wrapped in a paper bag, or went home for lunch. Our lunch hour was 12 'til 1. Everybody from Berry Down[16] would bring sandwiches.

Fred Spear was my particular friend; *he* was the one. We used to walk to my house on the Haggington Hill to have a cooked meal. My favourite was chicken and vegetables. Whatever was going he used to have. He used to bring his sandwiches; he didn't carry a lot, but these were extra. He knew he'd be all right with me!

---

16 Berry Down is 2.5 miles from Berrynarbor.

Berrynarbor School, 1925. Back Row L to R: Stanley Jones, Lily Ley, Rhoda Challacombe, Vera Latham, Muriel Richards, Doris Dinnicombe, Annie Seldon, Myrtle Richards, Ivy Watkins. Middle Row L to R: Lily Harding, Ephraim Street, Lionel Dummett, Albert Irwin, Rachel Irwin, Verna Richards, Muriel Yeo. Front Row L to R: Albert Adams, Reg Sydenham, Reg Toms: Ron's cousin, Reg Ley, Leonard Dummett, Vera Richards, Vera Ley.

Berrynarbor School, 1926. 'Probably taken at the back of the school in the school yard'. Back row L to R: Louis Smith, Ron Toms, George Irwin, Alfred Nichols, Reg Ley, Joe Huxtable, Ron's 'mate' Fred Spear, Lionel Dummett. Middle row L to R: Bill Irwin, John Hockridge, Rachel Irwin, Verna Richards, Vera Ley, Lily Huxtable, Frank Huxtable, Reg Toms. Seated L to R: Honour Irwin, Vera Dummett, Lily Tucker, Headteacher: Miss Veale, sisters: Freda, Brenda and Vera Richards.

SCHOOLDAYS AND CHILDHOOD CHRISTMASES

We had two Tortoise stoves.[17] One was in the room that was divided and one was in the other room. They had guards around them. We didn't have any hot water unless it was boiled on the Tortoise stove. It took a bit of time mind you, but it was the same everywhere.

We all walked to school then. Most of us, about fifty or so, were from around here. About nine or ten were from Berry Down. The children walked together from here; they *had to*, in *all* weathers.

If it was wet, our heavy, soaked overcoats would be put over the guards to dry. The children from Berry Down could be *very* wet. On *really* wet days, the room would be *really* steamy and smell of drying clothes, but sometimes they'd have to put them back on and they were *still* damp!

Our nailed boots that we wore would be put there too. All the boys wore these boots that came above the ankles; the girls from the farms wore them too but the other girls wore heavy leather, tough shoes: all low-heeled and made to last.

Sometimes, if it was really bad, George Harding, who lived in Berry Down, would bring his gypsy caravan down to Berry. When he had a job to do in the village, he'd come down with the children before 9am for them to go to school on time. He'd leave the caravan somewhere in the village and fix up the farm butt[18] to his horse to do what he had to do. He worked for the council and sometimes would leave the butt for a day or two to do work here. If he could, he'd take the children home in the caravan in the afternoon.

A stream runs under and crosses the road [in front of Briar Cottage, Silver Street] to the back of the school. There used to be two wooden seats, all covered in, over the stream, at the back of the school, facing Bessemer Thatch. There was a partition between: one for the girls and one for the boys; and the stream took everything away.

We would put our hands up and ask, "Please Miss, can I leave the room?" She'd know why, but only one was allowed to go at a time, so if a boy had gone and a girl asked to leave the room, *she* had to wait!

Newspaper was cut up into squares; this was our toilet paper! There was a nail on the back of the door for it. The papers were softer in them days.

If a girl was in the toilet at play-time, we used to get a bamboo cane... with its leaves on! We used to bend them so we could put it under the door and tickle her legs and that!

The school playground, 2012.

Our playground went *all* the way up to the school. It was bigger than it is now. The playground was divided: part for the girls and part for the boys. It was concrete that had one swing set into it, so if you fell off you could hurt yourself. There was a fence between the playground and the garden.

Where the playground is now there was a garden in five sections, which went down to the stream. On Wednesday afternoons, the girls used to plant flowers in the borders around the edges; the girls looked after these. Two boys would work in each plot: one was the 'Head'. We planted in the busy time, the summer, and then we'd dig it over and leave it. We never went out there when it was *very* cold.'

Ron's timetable excluded school excursions; however, decades later, Berrynarbor schoolchildren, like others up and down the country, did assemble, excitedly, for an educational visit or 'a day off school'!

Ron remembers 'Muriel Lucy Richards' the pupil, then her return to the school as 'Miss Muriel Richards' the student teacher. All of her working life was at Berrynarbor School. We see her in the photo overleaf surrounded by some of her pupils. The photo shows too that the children were no longer expected to sit, as Ron had, in formal rows, at 'double desks with lift-up lids', nor were they wearing a uniform that the children wear today.

'We didn't have any playground equipment. If we brought toys they'd be what your grandfather or father had made; they were always wooden.

We brought our marbles to play matches too. We

---

17 Charles Portway of Halstead, Essex, hand-built the first of thse stoves in 1830; they were manufactured in their thousands because the solid fuel burned extremely slowly and provided an economical heat. The burn pace gave them their name. The stove's top included a reptile image surrounded by the words 'Slow But Sure'.
18 'It was a solid wooden 'box' on a proper wooden frame, on two wheels, with a tailboard at the back. The shafts of the horse would be fixed to the frame. The butt's tailboard could be taken off to get the manure or mangels out. You could add extra sides to make it higher to take more. You'd have to load it so that nothing fell off or out.'

Schoolchildren's Outing early 60s. Mrs Cooperthwaite, School Head at the time of this winter gathering, stands on the right-hand side, to the left of the boy in his cap. Mrs Bett Richards is on the lowest step, to the right of the little girl at the end of the line, believed to be June Greenaway. To her immediate left is unknown, but left again, is ? Lowe. The smallest and youngest child, standing centrally, is Clive Richards, in front of his elder brother, Michael. Next but one is Anthony Rice; Rachel Fanner is to the right. She holds the arm of Paul Bowden. Above and behind Rachel is teacher Miss Richards.

Miss Muriel Richards with children in a maths lesson, probably early 1970s. L. to R: Tanya Walls, and behind, Elaine Stanbury, ? Pedlar, ? Irwin, unknown, then Miss Richards and Caroline Braine. On the left, seated, is unknown, but next to him is John Froud then Janet Fanner.

◈ SCHOOLDAYS AND CHILDHOOD CHRISTMASES ◈

used to get lemonade bottles that had marbles in the top. You could buy the bottles of lemonade. We'd break the bottles to get the marbles out. A lot of marbles were played then.

You could buy marbles: big and small. The big one was called the Jack. There used to be pretty marbles that had coloured streaks in them. We'd put the Jack down and try and hit it.

Sometimes we went over to The Globe;[19] we weren't supposed to, but if there were empty bottles outside, we used to take them and smash the neck to get the marble.

We'd make up our own games, such as 'Hats'. You'd line up your caps in a row and throw a ball. Whichever cap the ball landed in, it was the owner's turn to throw the next ball.

We had fun at school, but we had our differences too. Sometimes I had fights with other boys, up by the Old Rectory. I never saw the girls fight.

I wasn't sporty, but any sports were played on Parson's Meadows, near Orchard House: up the path by the side of Berrynarbor Park.[20] It was two long meadows, divided, and the Rectory owned it. We played football here. I did play, but I didn't know the first thing about it, but if we kicked the ball and it went in the goal, we'd shout "Hurrah!" There were no rules really; we just played.

Louis Smith, he went to Berrynarbor School. They called him 'Whippet Smith'. When he ran a race, he could *really* run. He was as fast as a whippet. He wasn't a big, burly boy, but in any school races he usually won. His father, Ernest Smith, had Mill Farm.[21] Their land was where the camp site is now.[22]

Louis went on to Chaloner's School in Braunton.[23] It was a *higher* school than Berrynarbor. I think he went there and stayed for a week – like a boarding school. He probably had to, 'cause there weren't the cars then and the parents didn't have the time either: it was just horses and carts.

For birthdays, you might go to a friend's and you'd still help out. Perhaps you were more of a nuisance than anything else, but it was a bit different.

Above left: *Ye Olde Globe.* Harvey Barton, Bristol *The road outside this village pub is known as 'The Village', before it descends to become 'Pitt Hill'.* Above right: *'The Globe's Kitchen Bar, possibly 1920s or '30s.*

---

19 Ye Olde Globe was established as a public house in 1675, converted from a row of three cottages. These are reputed to date from about 1280. Masons' homes were required to work on the church, because it was 'enlarged in the 13th century.'
20 Berrynarbor Park: 'Residential and Holiday Homes'.
21 Kelly's Directory, 1939, describes this as 'The Millpark Farm'. This farm was next to Berrynarbor Corn Mill, now Berry Mill House.
22 Operating as 'Mill Park Devon Ltd Touring Caravan and Camping'.
23 The roadsign of 'Chaloners Road' is the only visible tribute to William Chaloner, the Braunton vicar who founded Chaloner's Endowed School in 1667. His investments allowed boys of all ages, from 'the trade and farmers', to be schooled once they had passed a test. The original school was at 'The Shambles, Darracott, in the parish of Georgeham' near Braunton; it moved in 1886 to where Braunton Fire Station is today and existed until 1948. Their Latin motto means, 'They can because they think they can.'

THE BOOK OF BERRYNARBOR

Above: *School Group of 1930.*

Right: *Front Cover of School's Magazine 1934.*

Left: *School Badge.*

Below: *Chaloner's Road, Braunton 1930.*
R.A.P. Co. Ltd., London.
©Photograph from the Tom Bartlett Collection, EX34 9SE

SCHOOLDAYS AND CHILDHOOD CHRISTMASES

We'd have a party, a few sandwiches and a bit of cake. We couldn't go anywhere else, we *couldn't*.'

Ron's outdoor games after school are both familiar and unfamiliar. The village roads were another 'playground', which is a reminder of the lack of traffic at this time and their undulating nature aided and abetted these games. A local craftsman assisted, imagination was used and recycling was present as well, but this term did not exist then, but they did it anyway! Ron was an animal lover from a small boy; his pets were an important and pleasing part of his life as well.

'We had to make up our own games. We used to get a long stick. We'd tie a piece of string to it. We'd hold the string, put the stick between our legs and pretend this was our horse! We used to do all sorts of things like this. You had to make things yourself, but you could copy off your mates too.

We played 'Hare and Hounds'. One person would hide and say 'eek, squeak or 'olly [holler] or else the dogs won't folly [follow]. The other players used this to become the 'Hounds'. 'Hide and Seek' was another favourite and we often played amongst the bamboo canes.

We had metal hoops and crooks made by a local blacksmith. It was Sam Harding when I was a boy. The crook was the same height as the hoop. You held the crook and put the hooked end under the wheel and kept it going. We used to run miles with it: all around the village, uphill and down.

We used to go to the dump; the nearest was in Bament's Wood.[24] People would dump iron wheels, small ones: old pram wheels and that. We'd use them for our trolleys.

We'd make an edge to it, perhaps from an old wooden box, to keep you on it. This would be our seat. We'd steer it with rope. There'd be a small axle underneath with a bolt through the middle of it. The back wheels were bigger than the front but the back ones wouldn't turn; they'd follow the front. We made brakes: a wooden block. They were screwed to the side of the trolley and we used a lever to stop. We had to be prepared to put our feet down to slow it down too, but we had our nailed boots on.

If my stepfather said he wanted my help, he'd send my mates away, "He's not coming out; I want him today." You couldn't always have a good time.

At home, I had a dog and a couple of cats. Trixie was a little white terrier, with brown ears. We had a hedge about four feet high. On a dry day, me mother used to put a sack or an old mat for her to lie on. When she saw me coming down Pitt Hill, she used to leap off the hedge, down the steps and come down to meet me. She *was* pleased to see me!'

While he was still a schoolboy, Ron worked hard out of school hours too, as his stepfather was a 'taskmaster'. Additionally, he was expected to help in the holidays and at weekends.

As soon as he was 'about nine or ten' Ron helped out before his scholastic studies began; Ron and other pupils were 'milkmen' and he returned to Middle Lee to start his day. Their duties meant that they were allowed to arrive at 9.30am, but 'this was our deadline'.

He carried two, square, two-gallon cans of milk,[25] each had a cover and handle on the top. He used a pint jug to ladle this into his customers' jugs. 'One would be the skimmed and one would be the new'. The new milk was dearer. In 'old money' a pint of milk straight from the cow, was 'thruppence' [3d] or almost 2p in today's money.

After school Ron was expected to help with domestic chores such as cutting logs in the shed for the fires and to work in the garden; however, during the holidays he was also expected to work alongside his stepfather, Jack, and his working partner Joe Huxtable, to clear the local drains and roadsides of rubbish and mend the roads.

On Saturday mornings, he earned 'pocket money'. Ron and 'other lads' were given a shilling [1/- = 5p], for emptying toilet buckets, but in addition to his school week, he and other village children were expected to attend Sunday morning worship at the church and attend Sunday School in the afternoons, which was viewed as essential and an additional part of their education.

If he was a schoolboy today, paid employment would be impossible until he had reached thirteen years of age, and then it would be part-time only. During term-time, children may work a maximum of two hours on school days and Sundays and, on Saturdays, thirteen and fourteen-year-olds are restricted to five hours or eight hours when they reach fifteen or sixteen years of age.

In the holidays, at thirteen or fourteen, he would be allowed to work twenty-five hours a week only, which includes a maximum of five hours on weekdays and Saturdays and two hours on Sundays.

'Everybody *had* to be at school by 9.30am; if you didn't arrive at school by this time, a School Inspector would visit home. Bob Lynton would come out from Ilfracombe. My mum would send a note with the other children from the Hill if I was sick.

We had half a dozen cows: Devons. We kept one or two Jerseys or Guernseys and their milk was added to colour up the Devons' milk.

---

24 Bament's Wood is a narrow stretch of woodland, beginning near the A399 and ending near the coastline.
25 1 gallon = 8 pints or 4.55L

Bob Lynton on Pitt Hill with Haggington Hill sweeping upwards behind him, c.1900. Garratt, Bristol

The morning milk was straight from the cow, fresh, and delivered that morning. The afternoon's milk was all scalded. You'd scald it in a cloam[26] pan.

The pans were thick, round, brown pans, smaller at the bottom than the top. They had a thick edge around the top, just enough to hold. They were heavy for the ladies to lift, particularly when they were full: they'd take, probably, eight quarts: two gallons [9.1 litres]. We used them at Middle Lee and Home Barton.

The metal pans were used later. They had handles and they'd get *hot!*

The jug was put out the night before; it was mainly the older people. You knew where to take your milk, which customers you had. The cost was known too. It was a set price for years, so the money was left outside the houses in a pot or in a piece of paper; you knew everyday what they wanted. To my knowledge, no money was ever taken.

I'd start at Ducky Pool and delivered to the Streets opposite, at Rose Cottage. We didn't do every house, but by the time we'd delivered up The Village and in Lower Town and back down the hill, turned right and back to Lee, it'd be about fourteen or fifteen people. Didn't take long, they'd still be indoors; some might be asleep. The jug'd be upside down and a cup by its

Milk Delivery

side. Some would come out and say "Good morning" to you. They'd leave a ½ pint or 1-pint jug outside; you'd have a pint measure but you'd have to guess ½ pint if they'd left a 1-pint jug and wanted half.

The can had a section for the cream, but this was a luxury so it was only delivered at weekends, as it was double the cost of milk: six old pennies for a ¼ lb [2½ p for 4 ounces, or 113g].

---

26 'Cloam', Southwestern English dialect: made of clay or earthenware.

SCHOOLDAYS AND CHILDHOOD CHRISTMASES

People left their cups outside for the cream; sometimes they were handleless, but they were clean. It didn't matter. People throw them away today!

Payment was at the end of the week. Money was always paid on time. A lot of them were widowed and didn't have a lot, but we *never* worried about if we were going to be paid.

When I was a bit older, probably about ten or eleven, I liked to 'help' on farms... probably more of a nuisance really! I used to help move the milking cows from Mr William Huxtable's farm, North Lee; he rented fields all over. I know he rented at the back of North Lee, what is the recreation ground, and Pugsley's field.

We used to move the cows from North Lee farm along past Middle Lee and South Lee and we had to let them have their fill when they went into the stream, near South Lee; they'd be up to their knees! It was a deep stream then.

Then we'd take them up through Blind Lane, by the Rectory, and up Ridge Hill to fields on the right. We had to bring them home to milk them.

Sometimes, Mr William Bowden's cows from South Lee would join them, at the same time, for a drink, but when we wanted to move them on, the cows knew where they had to go! The cows of Mr Bowden would carry on to his fields; Rosy Park we called it.

We had to work during the holidays too. We had to do as we were told! If I didn't work on the roads in the holidays, I'd be up in the garden, digging the ground over.

The rubbish, from the roads was taken to a depot, a dump, on Fred Rice's field: off Ridge Hill and bear right past Bodstone [Farm]. Fred was Winston's grandfather. Winston's father was called Redvers; I went to school with him; and his younger brother, Denzil, went there too. Stowford Farm, Stowford Meadows,[27] has been in the Rice family for years.

My stepfather had a big garden: about five large plots. I had to help him. The garden went all the way to the top. Between 23 and the next one up [22], there's a bungalow there now and that space was ours too.

This was dug before winter, before Christmas, but you couldn't use anything else other than a fork. The frost would help to break up the ground. Then at a certain time of year, we'd plant it up with vegetables. I used to enjoy it. I liked being outside.

There was a right-of-way above Grattons which went to the back of the Haggington Hill gardens.[28] It only took you to a field, but you could turn round with a horse and a farm butt; if you wanted to take farmyard manure for the garden you could.

There were no flush toilets in them days and a shilling was a lot of money, but Frankie Challacombe

Berrynarbor Showing Haggington Hill, postcard dated sometime after 1937. Harvey Barton, Bristol

---
27 'Stowford Farm Meadows' is no longer a farm but another 'Caravan and Camping' site in North Devon.
28 There is a footpath or cart track 'above Grattons' that will take you behind 'Haggington Hill gardens', through woodland and on towards Hill Barton farm.

helped me. He lived up the Hill at 17. There was a door at the back of the toilet shed, a small door, big enough to get the bucket out. Then we'd dig a pit and bury it right away.'

To the left of the village's central clustered properties, can be seen a few houses on a hillside [see photo previous page]. Victorian maps show this as 'Haggington Hill' and, therefore, Ron's comment that it 'was always known as Henton' suggests that this is another dialectal example. The postcard illustrates his comment about 'large plots' and that 'people grew their own'. Since this date some of these plots have become properties and the modern road sign states that this is 'Haggington Hill'.

'The bus used to stop at the bottom of Pitt Hill, where the bus shelter is. There were more of them then and we knew when they were coming. They used to come round and through the village. It was a race between a couple of lads, me, Jack Snell and Frankie, to see who could get to the bus stop: to get to Mrs Bolton first; to get some money!

She lived in a big house 'Grattons' at the top of the Hill. She was getting on in years and stooped; we used to help take her groceries back up the Hill. The buses were the green and whites: the Southern Nationals.[29] They carried about twenty-five to thirty people and would travel along the Old Berrynarbor Road.[30]

The Southern Nationals were single [decker] in the beginning. They were on time in them days; you could rely on them. It'd cost about 11d [about 4.5p] return, from the church steps [Berrynarbor] to Ilfracombe, to the High Street. I think I was a boy then; I used to go in with me mother.

Later, the council used the double-deckers. They used the open-top bus to go round the village and cut the hedges, along Barton Lane and Pitt Hill. I've seen them do it! The main bus was the closed-in bus that took all the passengers.

They knew the times of the buses, so if they knew that another one was coming they'd pull in to one side: at the passing places. They'd stop anywhere in them days. You didn't have to be at the stop; you could put your hand up...

I think one of the school teachers took the Sunday school; I don't think it was the Reverend Churchill. I first went to church at St Peter's and we had choir practice on a Thursday evening, about six o'clock for about an hour.

Waiting by Berrynarbor's church steps: A Southern National bus.

---

29 The 'apple green and cream' buses started work in 1929, because in 1928 the big four railway companies had been given statutory powers to invest in bus companies, and, therefore, the Southern Railway was able to take a 50% stake in the newly-formed Southern National Omnibus Company, with the other half owned by the National Omnibus & Transport Company. The 'Southern Nationals' existed until the 1970s.
30 This narrow, hilly road runs between Goosewell and the Hele/Heel/Corn Mill.

◈ SCHOOLDAYS AND CHILDHOOD CHRISTMASES ◈

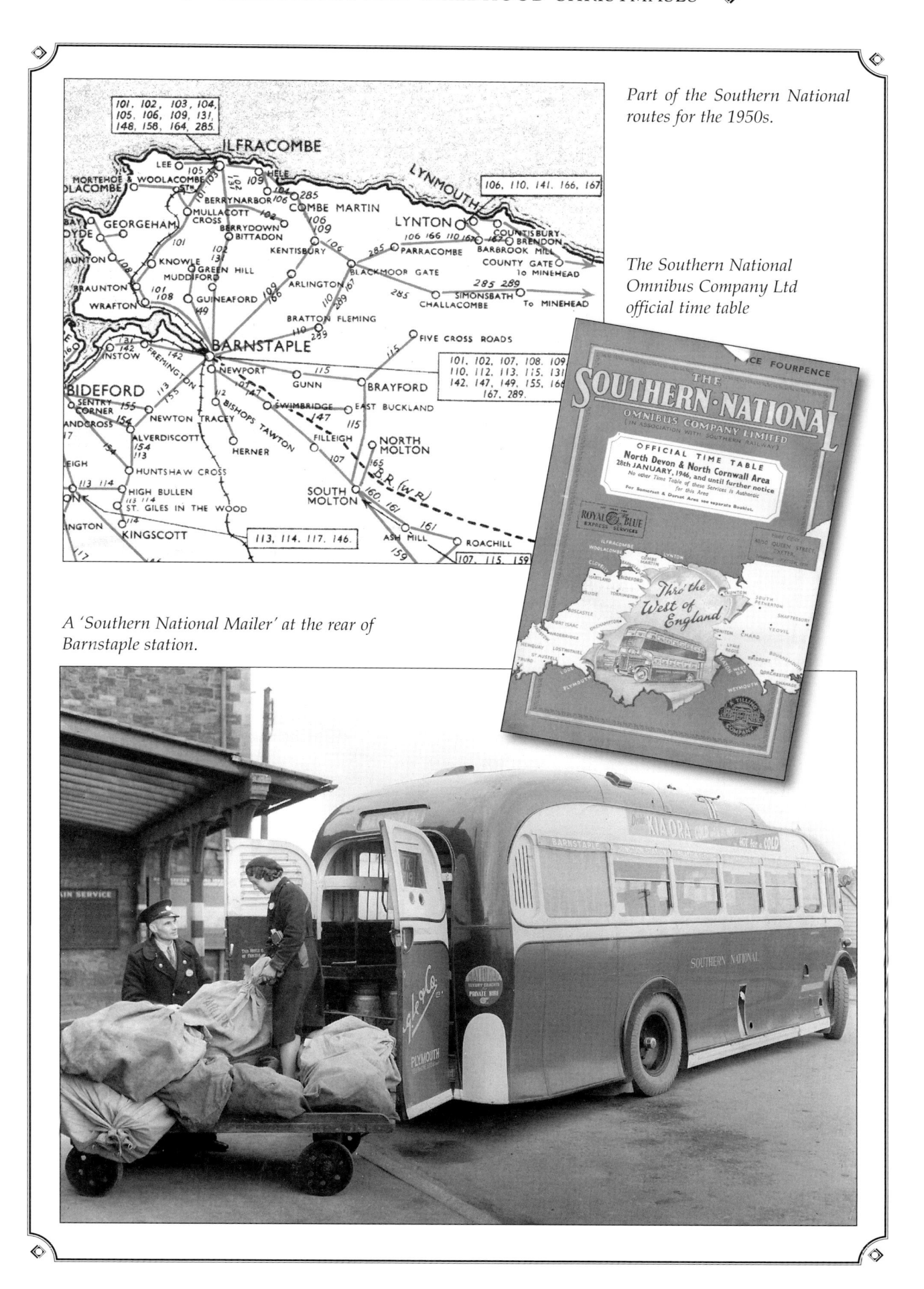

Part of the Southern National routes for the 1950s.

The Southern National Omnibus Company Ltd official time table

A 'Southern National Mailer' at the rear of Barnstaple station.

41

For a Sunday school treat, we would go to the Rectory; you took your mugs for a drink, and then you were given tea; we sat on the lawn if it was nice. For another treat, we'd have a ride in their horse and trap: from the Rectory to the end of the drive. After the horse and trap they had a car.

The Rector had two servants in the house all the time and two gardeners full-time and somebody to drive his carriage with his black horse, Gaiety it was.

Ernest Richards, John Huxtable's grandfather, looked after the key for the Parish Rooms and the key for the church. He worked for the Rectory and helped the Reverend Churchill. He used to drive the Reverend Churchill and his wife around in his horse and carriage.

Ern's brother, Dick, and Charlie Huxtable were the gardeners at The Rectory and it was a *big* garden. Before you pass between the rocks, in the Sterridge, there's a double door that was used for a horse and cart with a load of manure. There's another entrance for the garden, a single door after the double doors.'[31]

In 1866, Kelly's Directory *commented that this 'very handsome parsonage, in the Gothic style... (was) built about five years back by the present rector.' Walter Fursdon B.A. was the Rector between 1860 and 1876.*

Right: *Berrynarbor Rectory, 2012.*

Below: *Berrynarbor Rectory c.1910.* Garratt, Bristol

---

31 These doors no longer exist.

SCHOOLDAYS AND CHILDHOOD CHRISTMASES

Days before the Christmas of 1923, and while Ron was still a schoolboy, Ron's mother, Hilda Mary Toms, married George Henry Geen. He became Ron's stepfather and moved them from Middle Lee to Haggington Hill.

'Before he was married, he'd worked for a farmer who was also called George: George Nott of Combe Martin. He'd asked him if he could change his name. As he was the Boss, I should think he said he didn't mind; so he called him Jack. The Reverend Churchill always called him John, but everybody else called him Jack!

Jack wasn't born in the village; he was born in Hele. He went to the school there. The school was in the building opposite where the gas works was, where they sell cement and that today.[32] I think the school was there after it was a church.

Me stepfather was working at East Haggington Farm when they married. He took a farm cart to collect their bits of furniture and moved us to 23 Haggington Hill.

When we moved to Haggington me granny moved with us and so did Ernest for a while. There were only three bedrooms on the Hill, so I slept with me granny until she died. Ernest died before me granny.

Left: *Hilda Geen with neighbour Lorna Richards.*

Below: *Hele Bathing Cove, Ilfracombe.*

---

[32] 'Cement and that' can be bought from one of Rawle, Gammon & Baker Building Supplies' premises (RGBs).

Greta, my younger sister, was nine years younger than me.[33] She was born here. I can remember me granny with her foot on her wooden cradle rocking her and she'd be knitting or I'd be helping her: holding the wool around my arms while she wound it into balls.

When Greta was a baby and teething, me mother would sit her in the cradle. She'd give her a crust of bread to chew on to help her with her teeth.

Me granny was a midwife; *anyone* could be a midwife then. I used to go with her on different farms... in the holidays... not schooldays! Me granny and I would stay for a few days, when she was called on. It was a bit of a holiday for me. The doctors would come out when my children were born: Raymond and Sheila.

Christmas time was a bit different from what it is now too. The schoolchildren put on a nativity play at Christmas. Father Christmas would give out presents after the play. They were small presents, but the children thought they were wonderful I was Father Christmas once!

Left: *Small and tall: friends and neighbours Greta Geen and Margaret Grove-Price.*

Below: *A children's christmas party in Berrynarbor's Manor Hall.*

---

33 Greta's birth date was the 9th June 1925; she died in 2011. Margaret's was 16th June 1924 and she died in 2008.

SCHOOLDAYS AND CHILDHOOD CHRISTMASES

We had tinsel and paper chains at school. We made the chains at school but were allowed to take them home.'

In the, undated, photograph on the previous page we see tinsel and paper chains adorning the hall again. Ron is one of the adult helpers here, standing, with paper hat, to the right of the mirror but to the left of the small picture frame on the back wall.

Other helpers, beginning from the extreme left are: Ivy and Heather Jones: mother and daughter, Phyllis Watkins, Muriel Richards then an unknown; sisters Brenda and Vera Richards stand together in front of another unknown face. To their right is Rita Smith; Dolly Harding stands to the left of Ron. Bruce Stanbury stands next to him. Another mother and daughter, Rosie and Pam Brookman, stand in front of Ron.

The children are numerous, but names are not; however, Ivy Richards' daughter is the fourth face on the left-hand side of the table on the left and opposite her is Gordon Stanbury.

At the end of the front table is William, Bill, Huxtable. Gary Huxtable is between him and Wilfred Toms: Ron's cousin. To Wilfred's left is Bill's twin brother, Ivan. Kenny Richards is between Ivan and Brian Irwin.

'They didn't grow any Christmas trees for sale then but people wouldn't mind then what tree you cut. You'd go into the woods and cut one but it wouldn't be a fir tree, it'd be a holly tree. We wouldn't take a whole tree, just a nice-shaped branch; my stepdad would do it, but it'd be me mother that would put it in a bowl or a big bucket of earth. There weren't any presents on it and we'd have lots of holly to decorate the house too.

At home, we had small twisted coloured candles that were in holders; these had a clip and we clipped these on to the flattest branch of the tree. We used to put a cracker on or two. You didn't use to get the decorations that you do now. Our baubles were glass.

We used to *believe* it was Father Christmas. The stockings were as long as your mother's leg! At the bottom, there was an orange or an apple, a small bunch of grapes, just a few, and some loose nuts, walnuts and hazel nuts and a few sweets. We might have a homemade toy as well. The stockings were always on the end of your bed, when *you'd* gone to bed.

We'd all go to the village church on Christmas morning. I sang in the choir on Christmas morning, but you had to go in them days; that was the thing. If your mother and father said you had to go, you *had* to go. You *had* to do it. You *couldn't* say no.

Then we'd have our turkey dinner. It was special then; it was usually a turkey or it could be a goose. Christmas afternoon was quiet, mainly a family occasion: the adults would play cards and we'd eat nuts and sweets.

At the right time of year we used to go and collect nuts in the village. We'd get an ordinary 2lb jar [almost a kilo]. We'd fill it with nuts. We'd put some salt in with the nuts; then we'd dig a hole in the garden and bury it. We'd put a stick by it, so we'd know where it was. We'd leave it until Christmas; they were really good by then.

We used to play cards and games at Christmas, but I didn't. I used to eat the nuts, but they were meant for the card players!

On Boxing Day, in the daylight, the men of the village used to meet together and do rabbiting on farms and shooting. They'd have a couple of dogs with them; if they saw a rabbit run away they'd get it, but the rabbits didn't suffer.'

◇ ◇ ◇

Chapter 3

'Henton Hill', the Village and Nearby

This Edwardian family and friends gathering on the 'Hill', was some years before it became Ron's second home, but it is still recognisable even though more than a century has elapsed. The Hill is an excellent viewpoint for the church and its surrounding properties.

His description of this home at '23' was yet another startling reminder of contrasts: between his childhood home and those of today's schoolchildren. It is possible to see those similar to his home at open-air museums, such as St Fagans, Cardiff and in National Trust properties. Their exhibits are visible examples of how our homes have progressed over the centuries.

Ron's mother and other villagers had to collect water from roadside taps for every purpose. In walls at ground level, arched indentations around the village, such as at Church Corner, in Silver Street and on 'Henton Hill' show where these collections occurred.

Ron remembered that Sundays were important to particular visitors and when it came to doing the laundry, the next day was '*always*' washday. Washing machines were inventions of the future, so his mother and millions of others up and down the country had the same strenuous and lengthy task.

'I don't think all of these people lived on the Hill. Tommy Toms, my great uncle, and his wife Bessie, lived next door. They had three boys and four or five girls: there was Leonard, Stanley and Walter, and then there was Ada, Phyllis, Fanny and Edith; there may have been another.'

In looking at the photo below, Ron's memory serves him

Victorian and Edwardian children playing 'oranges and lemons' on Henton Hill, Berrynarbor.
©Photograph from the Tom Bartlett Collection, EX34 9SE

'HENTON HILL', THE VILLAGE AND NEARBY

well, as several members of the Toms family were present. Holding the arch were Florrie Ley[34] and Ada Toms. Under, and approaching the arch, were: Marjorie Jones, Cecil Toms, Albert Latham, Doris Richards, Fanny Toms, Freda Ley, Lorna Richards, Edie Toms and Polly Latham. Watching were: Tommy's wife with Leonard, Mrs Ley with Johnnie and Emily Ley.

'When I was a boy, we had another neighbour, Nellie Dinnicombe her name was. *She had a temper,* but there's always two to blame! When *she* was cross, she'd throw the early morning tea over the wall, over her husband below, as he was going to work. Then she'd walk to and fro, holding the clothes line, up and down again and again, shouting and screaming. We never knew what she said!

Number 23 begins just on the right of the pipe in the wall. It was a one-up, one-down with a lean-to shed at the back; this was the kitchen.

My mother cooked on an old-fashioned black leaded range; it was the Bodley.[35] The oven was at the side and the fire was next to it: to keep the oven hot. We'd put the irons on here to get hot.

We had candles, paraffin lamps and a gas lamp but no running water. We had a long tin bath with handles at the ends; they were kept in the back house, the kitchen. We had a bath in front of the fire. Water was boiled on the stove and we all used the same water. You took a pot to bed. We used the taps in the road for our water.

We had slab stones[36] and we had to wash them, on our knees; if it were clean today they'd go over it again tomorrow. We had brushes – no 'oovers then.

We had the electric light when I was about fourteen. Home was comfy: open grates for coal and logs, no electric fires, but we spent the summer outside.

We had to go up fourteen steps to the lavatory in the garden. It was in a wooden shed.

Instead of sweeping the chimneys with a brush, you'd tie a long rope to some holly. There'd be one person on the top of the chimney and one at the bottom and you'd pull it up and down to move the soot. When pulling it up, it was harder to pull, but it worked well. It was a job for men not for boys up on the roofs. We never used guards; I don't know of any accidents.

Soot's good for the garden; if you had slugs you'd put a circle of soot around and the slugs wouldn't go through that. It was a good fertiliser too!

All washing was done by hand. We had soap and soap flakes. 'Puritan' was a green block of soap. There was no washing-up liquid. Soap was used for dishes and clothes. The red soap was used for washing yourself: your face and that. I can't remember if this was Puritan too.

Clothes, bedding and tablecloths all went into a square tub. In the corner there was a place for the soap. You rubbed the soap across the clothes. Then the clothes were scrubbed with a brush, washed and rinsed. We used a washboard, part of this sat in the tub and then clothes were rubbed against it. We then squeezed them through a mangle to get the water out.

We had the weather then, so in summer it went outside. If it was dry in winter it went outside. Otherwise we used a clothes-horse: an airer. If a tablecloth wasn't dry, you'd put newspaper on the table. People didn't have the money to buy lots of cloths, so you'd have to put your plate on a bit of newspaper. People didn't mind then.

There were no electric irons. We had heavy, old-fashioned flat irons.[37] You had several because you used one while the others were heating up.

My mother used to bring it close to her mouth and

---

34 Florrie (Florence) Ley was the oldest child here; her birth date was registered as: 12.07.1895 with Johnnie being the youngest: 14.01.1905.
35 During the Industrial Revolution, foundries, nationwide, produced their own ranges and, often, proudly adding badges to display their manufactured location. George Bodley was a Devon iron founder; he patented his 'Kitchener' range in 1802.
36 'slab': broad flat thick pieces of stone.
37 Sizes, shapes and weights of these varied, but, on average, they weighed about 4.5 lbs, about 2 kilograms. They could be heated on a fire or range and were known as 'sad irons': 'sad' meaning 'heavy'.

St Peter's Church, Berrynarbor. Harvey Barton, Bristol

St Peter's Church, 1923. © Photograph from the Tom Bartlett Collection, EX34 9SE
This view shows its proximity to the Manor House and Manor Hall.

'HENTON HILL', THE VILLAGE AND NEARBY

Choir Outing, Woolacombe, 1913. Back row: *Dick Richards, Jack Bradford, Mrs Neals, E. Hicks, B. Harding, Rev. Churchill, H. Bowden, G. Goss, Rosie Bray, Glen Toms, Tom Ley, Ern Richards.* Middle row: *Mr Neals, Lorna Richards, Lily Richards, M. Pearce, B. Bowden, Dora Bradford, Lizzie Rice, M White, Lily Bowden.* Front row: *Jack Brooks, Sidney Dummett kneels between Jack Brooks and Will Bradford, Jack Richards, Ernie Leworthy, Percy Jones.*

give it a small spit to see if it was hot enough. She'd wipe it off and then iron the clothes.

Tramps used to come round the village begging, mainly on a Sunday; roadsters we'd call them. One used to come to me mother's when we were on the Hill. Before she would give him anything, she'd make him sing a hymn – he had a good voice – then she'd take him some sandwiches.'

The first church on this site was 'almost certainly' built as a 'small and low cruciform church of Saxon origin'. The rebuilt church, the Parish Church of St Peter, is part-Norman and part-13th century; however, two Chancel windows are believed to date from Saxon times. It is a Grade II* building. Its 'imposing Tower is approximately 96 feet high' [29.9m] and 'one of the finest in North Devon' that is of 'late Perpendicular date (about 1483)'.

Thirteenth century documents do not exist, but The North Devon Record Office, at Barnstaple Library, does have the registers for Christenings, Marriages and Deaths belonging to St Peter's from the 1500s: King Henry VIII's reign.

The Revered Churchill[38] was a significant figure in the village for more than half a century. Ron has fond memo-

ries of this man. 'He was a lovely person, the Reverend Churchill...'

Thus far, he is one of more than forty 'Rectors of Berrynarbor' who have served the community since Nicholas De Plymptone in 1261. He was well regarded apparently; his many years of devotion are commemorated in one of the few wall plaques in St Peter's.

TO THE
BELOVED MEMORY OF
REGINALD CHURCHILL
RECTOR OF THIS PARISH
1884-1938
DIED 21 DECEMBER 1941
AND OF
CAROLINE HARRIOT
HIS WIFE
DIED 14 AUGUST 1932

'The church was all lit by paraffin lamps. They had six or eight on stands; it's a long church.[39] The lights were up high; they were above people's heads, so you needed ladders to light them. They were

---

38 The Reverend Reginald Churchill was a vicar's son: William Churchill, Rector of Stickland, Dorset. Reverend Churchill served Berrynarbor until he was 85 years of age. He died in Braunton on 21 December 1941 at the age of 88, but was buried in Berrynarbor's churchyard on Christmas Eve, 1941. His gravestone commemorates his wife and their only child, Elsie.
39 It is in length and breadth about 75ft x 34ft, or 22.8m x 10.3m.

Interior of Berrynarbor church. Raphael Tuck & Sons

always wooden ladders then. They would be by every fifth or sixth pew, from the back of the church to the front. They had a couple in the belfry too.'

Part of Wild Violets, on Rock Hill, was a laundry. It was owned by the Rectory. This was glebe land; so was Orchard House.[40] The Rectory owned or rented quite a few fields round here.

On a Monday, Fred Spear's mother used to walk from Berry Down to their laundry and walked home. There was a lot of laundry for the Rectory; they had two servants living in that I know of. It was all washed by hand and then put through a mangle. It was dried outside on a long line.

There was a lady who was living in the house by the side, she'd bring it in. The weather was better then and they would iron it together, on Thursdays usually.'

One of the properties nestling beneath the church tower is 51 The Village, known as Tower Cottage. The Watermouth Estate sale documents list 41 properties for sale, apart from The Globe and Court Cottage, all are numbered; however, since this sale, numbering on many Slated Cottages has disappeared and many are now named; some display both. Additionally, parts of 'Large Garden(s)' have been sold off and thus property in a road has increased and the numbering altered.

In close proximity to Tower Cottage are the Men's Institute and Manor Hall.[41] The latter is one of several Grade II Listed village buildings that also include Old Court[42] and Manor Cottage.[43]

'All the village properties were numbered: when I was a boy and when I was married. Reg Ley was born at Hole Farm. He said there were three houses down towards Hele, past Hole Farm, that were numbered. The cottages, the Berrynarbor side of the stream, when you come up the Old Barnstaple Road, near the Hele Mill,[44] were where the numbering began and then it continued along Goosewell.'

---

40 'glebe: land granted to a clergyman as part of his benefice.' 'White's *Devonshire Directory* 1878' stated that 'there is a glebe of 126.5 acres'. Middle Lee acreage was 30acres less.
41 The left-hand side of this L-shaped building was built in the 14th century; the Men's Institute is here. The larger section on the right was an early Georgian extension and completed in 1914 and is known as the Manor Hall, used for events such as shows, parties and meetings.
42 Part of this is said to be from 'George III's reign': a Hanoverian and our longest-reigning king, 1760-1820.
43 Described as a '17th century Devon Longhouse'.
44 'It is recorded that Lord Fitzwarren built a mill at this site, Hele Myll, in 1525'. It was rescued from dereliction in 1973 and became fully operational again, grinding flour, with the help of its 18' Overshot Water Wheel.

◈ 'HENTON HILL', THE VILLAGE AND NEARBY ◈

Hele Mill before renovation c.1970s.

Hele Mill, 2012.

Right: *Hele Mill water wheel, 2012.*

Below: *Hele Mill water wheel, early 19th century.*

◈ 'HENTON HILL', THE VILLAGE AND NEARBY ◈

Drawing of the Manor House, 1861.

He wasn't related to the Leys at Tower Cottage, but mother and father [here] were Mary and Charlie, parents of Fred, Reg, Laura, Lily and Maud. There was another, Tommy, but he died at a young age. He must have been about nine or ten, but he was put in a big 'cot' in the garden. The garden wasn't as big as it is today. It was all open, no hedge at the front. They fenced a piece of the garden off, so he could hold on to it. I don't know what happened to him mind, but he couldn't speak proper.

Me stepfather told me that a lady used to sell sacks of coal from the cottages and sheds that were here, before the Manor Hall was built and before my time mind.

There were proper outside toilets on the ground where the grass play area is. They were taken down too. The grass play area was a garden. Bill and Jack Draper worked it; I don't know who owned it. Dan Toms, my uncle, had it for a while, when he was at Dormer Café [Muffets Tearoom]. It became British Legion ground after that.

The road towards the Manor Hall wasn't a car park. This was full of bamboo canes. They were used at the school for the naughty children. The canes covered most of the area in front of the Manor Hall. We played hide and seek here.

There was only a path here wide enough for a horse and cart. It went towards the Institute, where the sign is now.

The door was at the end of the Institute building: the side. There was only billiards here then, in my schooldays, and a Committee Room at the end. There was no door at the front of the building.

The Men's Institute was there and has been for as long as I can remember. Dan Jones lived up the Sterridge Valley; he was the caretaker and you couldn't get in until he came with the key. There was no bar then; you'd just go up for a game of billiards. It was always billiards, no snooker in my day.'

In Berrynarbor, Sterridge Valley c.1904
©Photograph from the Tom Bartlett Collection, EX34 9SE

The view in the photograph above is described as '71 and 69 Sterridge Valley and tap house', provides a view of another part of the village and an example of name change. A Victorian map describes it as 'Storidge' but village signposts declare that it is the 'Sterridge Valley'. It was taken 12 years before Ron's arrival, but he said:

'It looked exactly the same when I was a boy. The Streets owned the house on the left. Dick, Jack and Lizanne never married and stayed at the house; the others, Dorcas, Kit, and Bill married but stayed in

Berrynarbor. Two of the sisters are present here: Elizabeth, known as Tilly and perhaps 'Lizanne' and Dorcas.

The tap house is on the right. I don't know why it was so big. Everybody nearby would have used the tap. Everywhere had taps outside.

The roads weren't busy; there were only horses and market carts in them days. The Streets had a market cart. Their land, behind the house, was used for vegetables and they took it into Ilfracombe to sell.

Me stepfather also told me about the limekiln[45] in Bament's Woods, up near where Napps[46] is now. I didn't know anything about it because it was closed down long before I went to work for Fred Richards.

The limestone was dug from the quarry near the saw mill [for agricultural and construction use] put in to the kiln, water was added, not too much water though, and the stone would 'melt'. When it rained it would start to bubble up and become hot. When it bubbled up it became smaller and lighter. You'd have to keep your boots off it and you'd have to watch your eyes – no health and safety then!

There was a big pit there; they didn't make it safe, but there was a fence around the top. The bullocks[47] used to break the fence: probably after the ivy. They weren't allowed in here, but they must've broken the fence and fell in. They had broken legs so they had to be shot.

Napps was just fields; they belonged to Home Barton too. All the land, on the left of Sea View, as you're coming up towards Barton Farm, belonged to Home Barton. All the land either side of the main road belonged to them and towards Ilfracombe, the woodlands and everything towards the saw mill: both sides was Barton's.'

A nearby neighbour of Ron's, at number 16, was the village policeman, P.C. Abrahams. 'He had a top hat with a brass top'. *He was respected, as Ron admitted that whenever they were* 'up to no good' *and saw him, they disappeared.*

'We used to sit on the beams at the top of the church steps, always in the evenings. It was *very* dark, no lamp posts then, and hide above the lych gates. We would tie some string to a doorknocker opposite, to the Bessemer Thatch[48] which was a couple of houses then, or to Dormer House. There weren't many cars in those days, so we would sit, hidden, and wait for something to happen. When a car came it pulled the string and the knocker would knock on the door.

Tap house and plaque, 2012.

---

45 This is on the 1889 map.
46 This is 'Napps Touring Holidays' for 'caravans, motor homes and tents'.
47 bullock: a gelded bull; steer.
48 Believed to have been derived from a former occupant: Bess Emery, whose name was merged over a period of time.

'HENTON HILL', THE VILLAGE AND NEARBY

Berrynarbor Church, pre First World War. Garratt, Bristol
Showing the beams, the church steps and the lych gates.

The collapse of the Old Ilfracombe Road, 1919, at Golden Cove.

Somebody would come out and look around. They'd say something like, "Hey, if you don't stop it, we'll tell the teacher." Then they'd break the string and slam the door! If a car didn't come, we'd pull it anyway. Children wouldn't take any notice if you said that today!

When we had the street lights they were lit by paraffin too. A Berrynarbor-born lad, William Street, married and moved to Ilfracombe. He used to light the street lights; this was his main job. He wasn't the only man to do it; it's a big place. He did the ones around Hele and the Chambercombe area. He was lighting them one night, the ladder moved away and he fell. He hurt his back and he couldn't work no more. He eventually died...'

It is hard to imagine Berrynarbor or any community today with few cars and without streetlamps. There were fewer houses, but more shops and services when Ron was a child. These and working farms have disappeared gradually; their premises have become homes or given 'change of use'. When he was 'about eleven or twelve', Mill Park, now a caravan site, was a 'small farm'. 'Henton Hill' has become 'Haggington Hill' officially and is not the only name change.

'There was a pub on the Old Coast Road[49] near the Sandy Cove Hotel, before my time mind. The road was used a lot by the market gardeners on their way to Ilfracombe and they'd have a drink there, but some of the road slipped away. When I was big enough I went down to see it. It was the main road then, but people could still use it with caution. You could get by; you'd have to keep the horse steady and keep moving, 'cos a lot of it went into the sea.

The pub became empty and derelict so Stanley Harding and I went down there and took lots of stones away to repair or build stone walls on the farm

---

49 Ron's reference to a 'pub' was 'an inn, used by smugglers who stored their smuggled goods in the cellars'.

[Home Barton]. The road kept crumbling, so when [this section of] the road couldn't be used any more we took stones from here too.

The garage owned by the teashop [adjacent to Muffet's Tearoom, Dormer House] hasn't always been a garage. It was an animal pound[50] when I was a schoolboy. You had to pay so much to take back your bullock, horse or sheep that had been roaming the village. Who had the money I don't know.

It was never Silver Street in my day, it was always known as Lower Town. From Wild Violets up to the Turn Round was known as Jan [John] Braggs Hill.[51]

There were no houses from the Parish Rooms right the way down to Blind Lane. This was all allotments; we called them tenements[52] then.

I think it was called 'Blind Lane' because it had a blind corner. It was all uneven and rocky. It's filled in now; a lot of work has been done with a tractor since... It's a lot wider than it used to be; it was just a footpath then: wide enough for cows.

Before the main road [A399] was built, there was a road into Berrynarbor from the woods across to Birdswell Lane. Mr and Mrs Alfred Leworthy and their family lived in Court Cottage in Birdswell, but there weren't many houses up Birdswell: all tenements here too.

Birdswell Cottages, where I used to live, were built as agricultural workers' cottages, and were new when I moved in. The war was still on then. My boss

Birdswell Cottages

was on the Agricultural Committee, so I probably stood a good chance of getting one.

I think they were owned by the council because a man would come round for the rent. They were very particular then: how you kept your house and your garden. You had to abide by the rules.

They were for the agricultural workers, but I was the only one who was when we moved in. There were other agricultural workers who lived in the village, but they lived in other cottages. Other younger married couples, moved in later; you all had to be married and they were all agricultural workers too.

This is the front of the cottages [photo below], probably taken from Haggington. The view's different, all covered in now by the trees.

Birdswell Cottages, surrounded by other properties

---

50 Animal pounds were used for strays or those seized in recompense for a debt or to enforce payment. Strays were rounded up by the 'Pinder'; he cared for all impounded until they were reclaimed and was paid for this office. A few remain, such as the 'later prehistoric' stone pound at Dunnabridge on Dartmoor, but their existence is often marked by names such as, 'Pound Hill', or 'Pound Lane'.
51 Censuses between of 1841-1901 state that three 'John Braggs' were born in 1796, 1816 and 1848 and lived at Hill's Cottage'. The Watermouth Estate sale documents include 'John Braggs Hill' and 'Hills Tenements'. The hill is now known as Rectory Hill.
52 'Tenement, *Property law* any form of permanent property, such as land, dwellings, offices, etc.'

'HENTON HILL', THE VILLAGE AND NEARBY

Berrynarbor Village. Foreground and left is Dunchideock, opposite the church wall. Bessemer Thatch is the only other clearly visible property.

When I was a boy, we used to walk along the path towards Birdswell; before Old Court there's a path. This was the back entrance to The Lodge. There was a stile at the bottom of that, that took you into a field, and you'd come out in Pitt Hill, opposite the recreation field. It's the big overgrown field with the gate at the bottom. This was known as Pugsley's field. I understood it that some people who'd owned it were Pugsley. It's part of Old Court now. Colonel Stoney and his wife lived there years ago.

Bessemer Thatch was a couple of houses before it was a hotel. My wife, Gladys, did the housework and helped with the children at the nursery in Bessemer [before it was a hotel]. She helped for a couple of days a week, but there was a nurse who was there all the time and a matron.

When I was at school, Dunchideock, 54 The Village [now The Shippen], was home to Mary Toms, but she wasn't a relation. She owned the land, 'Claude's Garden'[53] opposite the church. She had it well before it was 'Young Claude's'. She had a couple of sons and after she died one of them took it on. Dunchideock has a courtyard facing the road because Claude had a dairy here.

Before it was Claude's, Sam Harding, the wheelwright and blacksmith used to tie up the horses here, and any broken wheels on the carts would be repaired here. They were made here too. He lived at Hillcrest, [No 55].

The horses were shod opposite, near the school, beyond Miss Veale's. He sold the business to Harry Camp; I think Harry came from Kentisbury.[54]

There was always a cobbler in the village too. The one I went to was George Hobbs; he wasn't a local man; he came from Chittlehampton.[55] He was the postman as well. He was a friend of our family too. When he first came to our village he came to our house for his meals.

He was a postman in Ilfracombe. He'd ride his push bike there, sort out the letters, bring them back to the village then start his cobbling.

Before he married Marjorie Bowden, from the village, he would finish his round and come for a cup of tea or coffee with me mother and then he'd go back to his farm shed to do his cobbling, in one of the sheds opposite the farmhouse... North Lee.

Where the septic tank is now, at the bottom of the recreation field, there were two fenders: two large

---

53 This has an excellent viewpoint of the central village. ['Young'] Claude left it to the village of Berrynarbor in perpetuity, in memory of his parents, Fred and Emma Richards. Berrynarbor Parish Council own it.' It is part of the 'Quiet Garden' scheme.
54 A parish located about a 15-minute drive from Berrynarbor.
55 Chittlehampton to Berrynarbor is about 23 miles.

Views of and from Young Claude's Garden, 2012. The side of Hillcrest faces this garden. His seat, dedicated to him by his brothers and sisters, is closest to and overlooks three cottages; Dunchideock sits to their right, beneath this memorial space.

'HENTON HILL', THE VILLAGE AND NEARBY

George Hobbs delivering the post, 1930s.

The village of Chittlehampton, home of George Hobbs.

Berrynarbor Mill c.1904. © Photograph from the Tom Bartlett Collection, EX34 9SE

pieces of wood with a metal top. When the mill needed water the fenders were raised. The recreation field belonged to North Lee farm then.

The path and the stream [opposite North Lee] were wider than they are today and went from The Lees, near the bus shelter on Pitt Hill, under the bridge, through the garden at Rose Cottage and through the field, what is the caravan site now [Mill Park].

The mill was attached to the house [now] Berry Mill House.[56] Ernest Smith had the farm here. He lived in the mill house. He was Parky Smith's father. Parky's sister was Evelyn and their mother was Edie.

The farm wasn't a big farm, probably about 40 acres. The steep field between Hagginton Hill and Mill Lane belonged to them and the cottages in front of Berry Mill were farm buildings years ago.

Ern Smith was known as Miller Smith. He worked the mill and the farm. He wasn't a miller in a big way, but everybody had pigs then, perhaps two or three, so if you took a bag of corn down, he'd grind it for you. Their pigs were fed on ground corn, meal and boiled potatoes.

They'd be big pigs: thirteen or fourteen score,[57] *really* big pigs. They've only got to be five score today, so you can sell 'em. There are so many restrictions today, you mustn't do this; you mustn't do that, but there was nothing like that in my day.

Ern went from Mill Farm to West Haggington Farm; West Henton we'd call it. The Burgesses had it after the Smiths. I went to school with their daughters, Phyllis and Gladys Burgess[58] who lived here, but it was still a farm then. When he retired he went to live at Langleigh House.

---

56 Currently, this property operates as a guest house and a B & B, but 'Mill Park', Berry Mill, was recorded 'as a woodworking mill' in 1933 and 'as a mill wheel supplying electricity to Watermouth Castle' in 1934. Mill Park House was the original mill; Mill Park Cottage was the farmhouse, built in 1671. Tithe records of 1841, show a miller and maltster living in this farmhouse. Current owners say: 'The river [Sterridge] could be redirected down the mill leat; the water went across the road to work the mill.' It is also probable that this was the site for an earlier mill, as the villagers would have needed to have ground their corn.
57 'Old English *scora*; related to Old Norse *skor* notch, tally, twenty.' Ron added: 'it used to mean twenty pounds [weight] in my day.'
58 Kelly's, 1923, records that their father was 'Burgess, George, miller (water)'.

'HENTON HILL', THE VILLAGE AND NEARBY

Rear of Langleigh House: the three-storey Building.

Langleigh House below cottages; number 37, (38) Forge Cottage and Swan Cottage, 1940.
Reproduced from a F. Frith & Co. Postcard

The 'proper sawmill', Early 1900s. Uncertainty reigns, but those present are 'Alf Brooks, Will Delbridge, Harry Slee, Jack Ley and Dan Jones'. Holding the cross-cut saw are thought to be Alf, on the left, with Dan opposite.

When I was a boy, and a teenager, The Sawmills wasn't a pub; it was a proper sawmill. Tommy Toms, my great uncle, was a carpenter. He was the overseer there, but he did help sometimes. They'd have big trunks sawn into planks; it was sold to carpenters around here and the bits were used for fires for the family: the Penn Curzons.

The Penn Curzons owned Watermouth Castle, all the cottages on their estate and all the woodland towards Ilfracombe, on the left. Jack Ley was their manager.[59] Before them it was to the Bassets. You had to go to Jack's house to pay your rents. He lived in the first house up the track opposite the sawmill.[60]

Tommy and one of his sons, Leonard, worked there. One day, when Leonard was using the long saw, driven by a belt and worked by an engine, Leonard put his fingers too close and cut two or three off. He was probably only in his 30s. They rushed him to hospital: the Tyrrell[61] in Ilfracombe.

Logs were never *sold* to the villagers and the long planks were cut mainly for the farm buildings. We would use a cross-cut saw to cut trees then. If a tree had blown over we'd just help ourselves. We didn't have to *pay* for any wood then.

The sawmill's men would cut wood from the estate-owned trees and the Castle grounds, but it'd be the men from a firm in Ilfracombe, Ellis's, that would cut the others. Albert Jones, Jack Joslin and Dick Richards were all from the village and they'd go *miles* away, all around the woods. Their boss would go ahead a few days before and he'd mark a tree, so the men knew which one to cut.

There was a lot to it then: no electric saws. You had to cut all the branches off first so they'd go right down on their knees, with leather pads on, and pull the grass away so it was as close to the ground as they

---

59 Kelly's Directory, 1919, records that John 'Jack' Ley was the 'land steward to Mrs Basset, Watermouth castle'.
60 The 'track' is 'Mill Park Lane'.
61 Officially, this is The Ilfracombe and District Tyrrell Hospital, but is known as 'The Tyrrell' after its Victorian originator and supporter, Miss Ann Tyrrell. Born in 1802 in London, she moved to Ilfracombe in 1840. Cottage Hospitals began in 1859. At the time, on average, two a year were added, and, therefore, her cottage hospital of 1864 was an early one. She had leased two Horne Road cottages in 1863 and during the following February its first patients were admitted. The painting is believed to have been her 'sketch', shown to her builder in 1868 for the larger, 12-bed hospital. This was completed in 1870. She became its first 'Matron in Charge' and remained in this post until her death on 28th November 1875.

◈ 'HENTON HILL', THE VILLAGE AND NEARBY ◈

The Tyrrell Hospital; a sketch for Ann Tyrerell's builder.

The Tyrrell rear view c.1900-1910.

could get it. They leave a couple of feet *today!* They'd make a V-shape just up from the bottom, so it would fall the right way. All the wood had to go back to Ilfracombe to Mr Ellis's sawmill: at the back of the High Street somewhere.

They'd have two big, tall horses; they'd be in the wood, on a certain path. They'd clear it first. They'd be chained: long chains, around the tree and the horses. One chain'd be around the tree and that would be attached to another around the horses.

They'd pull the tree right down, through the woods and on to the road where they could get it loaded. There was a long wagon, long enough for the trees to go on. They'd put a couple of planks from the road up to the wagon and the horses would pull the trees on to the wagon using these chains, but the men had to wind up: reduce the length of the chain so that as the horses were pulling the tree would be moving into the wagon; the length of the chain had to be just right.

All the trunks were made fast on the wagon. They wouldn't slide out or anything if they were going up the hill, but there'd be no red flag at the back if they were hanging over the end.

The horses had to come from Ilfracombe because there were no stables big enough here. Once they'd done their day's work, they had to be walked home.

The house to the side of the pub wasn't there then, but there was a garage and a shed. Our neighbour, up the Hill, 22, Mr William Dinnicombe had it; we called him Bill. His wife was Nellie and they had two daughters, Doris and Ivy. He bought in coal, from somewhere, and sold it to villagers, delivered it around, when I was a boy. Ilfracombe market was on Wednesdays and Fridays, so he'd come round on a Tuesday evening collecting greens and potatoes with his horse and cart. He had paraffin lamps on the cart. He'd take them on behalf of others, for a bob or two. He'd be at the market, early: already there for people going in on the bus.

He helped Tom and Jack Ley. Jack was a builder, in a small way, and Bill used to take things, building materials in the horse and cart for them.

You could leave your rubbish, a bag of something, twice a week: a Monday and a Friday. He'd keep an eye out for it. He'd come round with a horse and cart. There wasn't so much rubbish from people; we only used paper bags or cardboard boxes then. I don't know how he was paid. He used to do a lot for the village.

The seagulls didn't come over the village so much then. They'd stay on the rocks near the sea. You didn't see so many inland as you do today; they're after the rubbish that's left, but you'd see them when you were ploughing though. They'd be after the worms: the big fat ones. They were bigger, *much* bigger, than garden worms, but they weren't so long; perhaps they were the caterpillars...?'

In 'Lower Town', when Ron was a child, the house next to the school, Cutts End, became a butcher's shop; the post office was here too. Ron's' school is still here.

Meat could be ordered from the butcher's and delivered to villagers, but like many other facilities, the blacksmiths[62] and butchers have gone.

'My favourite shop was in Lower Town. It wasn't a shop really; it was the blacksmith's: between the school and Little Gables.

Will Irwin farmed over at West Down. Before he had the butcher's shop, a butcher's van would come round. Frank Isaac had a shop in Ilfracombe and he'd bring the meat round every Friday evening. They'd take your order one week and deliver it the next.

The meat wouldn't be all chopped up in pieces ready for you. You'd go in and ask for what you wanted and they'd cut it up for you. It used to be wrapped up in newspaper, years ago.

The post office was always in that bow-fronted building; it joins Briar Cottage[62]. It moved for a while,

Berrynarbor c.1920-1924. T.I.C
Opposite the church steps is the beginning of Lower Town. The Post Office occupies the foreground. 'The whole building was for the post office.'

---

[62] *Kelly's Directory,* 1850, mentions 4, but in 1939 the position was held by George Henry Camp.

'HENTON HILL', THE VILLAGE AND NEARBY

used to walk through fields *and* gardens, nobody minded then. You could walk up by Lee Side, over the fields and you'd call in at Hill Barton and then you'd carry on and reach the Sterridge Valley Farm!

Every Thursday, my uncle, used to deliver the Journal,[63] up to Woolscott Farm: to Mr Huxtable, but papers were often posted then: to the outskirts. There was more farming news in it then; well there was more farms then!

Polly used to live in Briar Cottage, next to the Post Office. She used to take in washing too *and* do people a good turn. I think she married a Draper.

There was a man with a horse and cart who'd come round to people that did teas and he had bottles of lemonade and jars of cider; they were always cold.

You could buy lemonade powder in packets, too, from the Manor Stores. He'd have it loose, and you could buy ½oz [approx 14g] or 1 pennyworth [0.417p]. You took it home and added water to your taste.

The fish van used to bring fish and chips to sell from outside Miss Muffet's [Tea Rooms]. The Unicorn Inn[64] stood where The Lodge stands today; Fuchsia Cottage was a drapers; and [43] Flowerdew Cottage was the Manor Stores.'

As the village has existed for centuries, it has numerous homes built many years before the first Planning Act of 1909.[65] *It is to be expected that over the decades, all or most properties will have been altered in some way.*

The Manor Stores is a graphic example, as the original building is believed to be mid-18th century or older. In 1920 it was described as, 'Shops, Garden, Premises, Tiled 2-stall Stable, Coach House and Loft.' This central village

Road To Sterridge Valley. Garratt, Bristol
A postcard that was posted in the 30s.

for some reason, to Langleigh House, and then it moved back to Lower Town. It was there until it moved into the new village shop [opened March 2008].

They'd use red wax to seal the knots on the parcels then. They'd warm the wax with the candle; and you could send telegraphs from *here*! The whole building was for the post office.

My uncle Ernest was a postman in the village. There was a lady too: Polly Courtney. She'd go one way, around the saw mill and Watermouth Castle; she used to walk *miles*. He used to go another.

They had to walk everywhere and they used the shortcuts: quite a lot of them in Berrynarbor. They

Berrynarbor Village, 1940. The Manor Stores is on the left. Reproduced from a F. Frith & Co. Postcard

---

63 *North Devon Journal*: The first issue of this first North Devon newspaper was published on 2 July 1824.
64 *Kelly's Directory*, 1850, records that 'Thomas Kent' was the 'vict.' [victualler or innkeeper] of the 'Unicorn'.
65 This was the 'Housing and Town Planning Act 1909', but a House of Commons Written Answer (1912) mentioned that 'it has been of very little use in rural districts.' It wasn't until 1932 that legislation included the 'Town and Country Planning Act'. The 'Town and Country Planning Act 1947' repealed all previous Acts.

The Manor Stores, 1970s. J. Arthur Dixon
from a composite of Berrynarbor

Flowerdew Cottage, 2012. 'The Manor Stores'.

space was viewed, obviously, as a viable business venue. A Victorian extension was added to the original. A trap door is still present and part of the flooring of this first-floor room, suggesting that this was the 'Loft' for the hay, above the 'Stable'.

Currently, the 'Stores' façade implies that the entire 'Premises' are part of a curving terrace that begins in Silver Street; however, a further recent find has been a tiny window, complete with its limewashed stone surrounds and visible hand-cut saw marks on its asymmetrical oak lintel, in a thick internal wall. On this site, seemingly, this building began as part of a traditional, one-up, one-down cottage complete with inglenook fireplace and its bread oven, adjacent to others...

'It used to sell everything in the grocery line: paraffin... candles... matches... bacon... sugar... tea and soaps: the red and the green soaps, not the flakes or powders they have now.

The bacon wouldn't be ready for you. They'd put a big piece on a slab and they'd turn a handle and cut it into slices. They could alter the wheel so it could be thick or thin and you had as much as you wanted.

Cheese was always cut with a wire on a block. There was no variety; it was just English Cheddar. I don't think any farms round here made cheese, not that I know of anyway, so we just had Cheddar from the Stores.

They didn't sell vegetables or fruit because people grew their own, or went to the market in Ilfracombe, but if they had any extra it was taken to the shop to be sold, not to make money, so it didn't go to waste.

I used to go in to the shop on my way to school. I used to buy sweets. We weren't allowed to eat in class. If they saw your mouth working they'd say, "Take it out and put it in the bin." Jelly babies were my favourite then. When I was older I liked the nut chocolate.

The jelly babies were in jars in the shop. They'd make up a bag, with *newspaper*: a cone in their 'ands. They'd hold it and twist the bottom, so the sweets wouldn't fall out. As the years went by there'd be little white square paper bags instead.

Charlie Ewens owned the Stores when I was a boy, long time ago now.[66] Him and his wife ran it; she was one of the Huggins sisters: three little ladies. They ran the post office, opposite where the butcher was; it was *just* a post office then.

Charlie owned a small donkey and cart. Fred Ley was employed to do the deliveries; he was called 'Donkey Ley' – he didn't care for it mind! He had it before Alfred Baker.

When Alf took the Stores on, he had the place next door as well [39]. Strangely enough Alf was a baker; he baked the bread for sale at the Stores and *he* had a man work for him called Tom Baker!

A Miss Cooper had the Manor Stores once. She was a bit crippled and she had help in the shop and everyone liked her. She came into the village and when she retired she moved into the house next door, [46].

She sold wools, pins and cottons on the left of the front door of the Stores and on the right was the main shop. If they hadn't got it, they'd get it in. There wasn't so much in tins in them days.

Next door to the Stores [39, Blue Mist], was a store and a garage. It was the bakery before Harry Graves, the cobbler, took it on. The bakery was still here, but it wasn't used then. Harry would sit inside the double doors at the side of the house, facing the end of the Stores, selling papers from here and taking in

---

[66] At the time of the sale, 43 was 'in the occupation of Mr. C.F .Ewens (Grocer, &c) as a Quarterly Tenant.' His 'Tithe' was '3s.3d' or 16.25p in 'our' money.

'HENTON HILL', THE VILLAGE AND NEARBY

shoes for his cobbling. You could buy papers from the Stores as well. His wife delivered them all around the village in the morning.

They lived in a bungalow – Little Sanctuary, on Rectory Hill. Wooden built, good wood; it was always little! He did his cobbling in another little shed outside. He was also the caretaker at the Institute, but that was only open in the evenings.

Next door to Blue Mist is Swan Cottage. Years ago, that was a blacksmith's shop. Harry Camp moved to Forge Cottage and worked from next door. You could go down on the outside to the bottom of Swan and go across into Forge.'

The Bessemer Thatch was one of the thatched properties in the village. It was once a commercial property too, a hotel. The photograph seen below stirred more of Ron's memories and produced further descriptions of cultivation, social activities and information about 'his' village and nearby.

'It burnt when I was on the farm – in the 30s. On the night of the fire, we were moving bullocks: me and the Boss. He was in the car and I was on a pony; the dog was running behind. We'd taken them from Combe Martin and over towards Blackmoor Gate, past [near signs to] where the zoo is, to Coulsworthy Farm, Kentisbury, and the next junction on the left. He rented the grass here.

We used to take sheep there too, but not very often, 'cos it was a long way.[67] Someone told us, when passing through Combe Martin that it was on fire. It was a light night. Some say it was started by children with fireworks and there again I've heard that someone next door, number 46, had lit a fire and the wind blew the sparks.

Days later, Stan Harding and I took two horses and farm butts and went to collect all the burnt wood and ashes. We put it on the grass fields; ash is good for grass. You could certainly see where we'd put it!

Behind the big trees is Muffet's Teashop; when I was at school this was owned by Miss Bray. The trees were elms and started at the back of where the bus shelter is now. Probably about four trees, they were *really* big trees.

There was a lean-to, round the corner from the steps. It had a slate roof, so you could stand here and wait for the Southern Nationals, but a lot of people didn't bother with the bus. They'd use the horses and the carts or walk. They'd use the Haggington Hill

Berrynarbor c.1904. ©Photograph from the Tom Bartlett Collection, EX34 9SE
Bessemer Thatch and the church's cobbled steps

---

67 Coulsworthy to Home Barton is about 4.5miles. It is signed to 'Trentishoe' and 'Hunters Inn'.

and on to Hele. They'd have baskets, but it wouldn't be heavy stuff – flowers and what have you.

There was a driver and conductor on the bus. If you did have anything heavy, the conductor would take it for you. He'd take it up the steps and put in on top. He'd walk along the top of the bus, put things at the front, and then work back. It was a high enough rail around the top and it was all packed in tight.

They were very good: the conductors. I can name some of the drivers; they were mainly from Ilfracombe and Combe Martin. There was Bill Hicks (Will), Eric Squires, Bill Waldron, Gordon Willis, Ivor Darch and Norman Sloley. The steps going into the bus were high, so they'd carry a step stool. They'd help people on: take their arm…

The last bus would leave Ilfracombe at 11.00pm and come through the village, so there was no problem getting home and then it would go on to Combe Martin. The last bus would have a Combe Martin driver.

There was a cinema, the Scala[68], and it was near where Somerfields is.[69] The bus would be parked in a lay-by on the road, beyond the London Inn. We'd go to the cinema then have fish and chips at Conibear's. This was near Jeffrey's paper shop. We'd sit in the shop with our young lady, if we had one. Sometimes the bus would go past, but we didn't mind, we'd walk home. The buses would come through the village, even the double-deckers!'

In 1869, a London-based shop opened its doors to sell 'high-quality products at low prices'. This Drury Lane retailer was the forerunner of the thousands of supermarkets up and down the country today. Elsewhere, in towns and villages, nationwide, it was the family-owned specialist shops that served the public.

In addition to the village shops, Berrynarbor villagers were able to use the nearby coastal resorts of Ilfracombe and Combe Martin. Combe Martin has two beaches; its 'seaside' and the one shown in the photo opposite.

The number of people seen in the photo prove Ron to be correct that in the summer 'you knew they'd come'. What was Carey's market garden rises behind the holidaymakers.

This town and village have been an intrinsic part of Ron's life from childhood and the variety of businesses here meant that villagers did not need to go further afield as they could purchase their clothes, groceries, greengroceries and hardware from within this area. Freshly-caught fish, landed by local fisherman was also available.

At more than two miles long, Combe Martin is renowned for having England's longest high street. Ron can recall it bustling with businesses.[70]

'Me mother used the buses to do her shopping. They were more often then: about every hour.

The Scala.

The Clifton.

---

68 The Scala Cinema opened in Ilfracombe on Monday December 20th 1920. Its dancing saloon and café opened on Monday May 16th 1921. Built to add to the town's facilities, it became the third 'picture house'. 'The Palace Cinema' was also in the High Street, at the other end, and 'The Empire Cinema' was in Northfield Road; the words 'The Old Picture Hall' above a doorway indicate its location. The Scala was renamed the Gaumont on the 10th December 1949, which then became The Clifton Cinema on the 28th June 1964. The latter had two screens, but it was demolished in 1983.
69 Now the Co-op, Ilfracombe High Street.
70 A list for the 50s and 60s, compiled by Combe Martin Museum's volunteers, reveals that there were 95 shops and businesses, 'excluding builders' yards'. Currently there are 32.

'HENTON HILL', THE VILLAGE AND NEARBY

Newberry Beach, Combe Martin c.1955.
Reproduced from a F. Frith & Co Postcard

Advertising poster: Combe Martin

I can remember six butchers [in Combe Martin]. Sue's was a butcher's shop. It wasn't all a shop; some of it was residential.

There were six or seven bakers' shops including the present one, which has always been there as far as I can remember. The Parsons brothers had one shop each and used to deliver bread around Combe Martin and Berrynarbor. One was down by the seaside and one was just above the Methodist Church.

A horse and a covered-in bread van delivered it. You always had two men, because you couldn't leave the horse; some houses were well off the road.

Freda and John Sharpe had a dairy; they had the milk from her brother: Claude Richards. It was set back from the road, but in the same place as Scissors is now.

Woody's,[71] in my day, belonged to George Creek – a draper. He came to my parents at Middle Lee. He used to have a van with a driver. The driver stayed in the van and Mr Creek used to go into the houses with shirts, socks, pants, boots and shoes.

He'd go round the villages and always had a cuppa and was never in a rush to leave! He did a visit, once a fortnight probably, so you'd have to wait as there were no 'phones then. If he hadn't got something you wanted, he would bring it with him the next time.

There was a hardware shop, owned by Jack Sanders, which was before St Peter's Church[72] and beyond the village hall. He used to sell paraffin, nails and wellies and you could have your horses shod here. He used to deliver as well, with a horse and cart. He had a paraffin tank with a tap fitted into the cart. There were ironmongers and blacksmiths too.

Fishing boats used to catch herrings. People would wait by the seaside. Combe Martin folk would buy what they wanted and then the fishermen would come up to Berrynarbor. They'd stop at the church steps and shout, "Combe Martin herrings, fresh herrings." They used to salt them or you could have them fresh. They could be big or small.

When I was a boy, the nearest doctors lived in Combe Martin. The Doctors Manning were husband and wife. They lived near Church Corner.

You had to ride, your pushbike or your horse, to fetch one and then travel back with them to the patient.[73] They used their horses, black and grey, to travel around.'

In addition to the shops, this village has had a museum for about twenty years. Typically, Ron has donated; the

F. Creek Ironmongers c.1890s

first item he spotted was the 'Cows and Horses Drenching Bottle'. Stoneware flagons, photographs and postcards were other reminders.

'To drench was to give an animal its medicine. For a horse, you'd tie string around its moustache, its jib, jibber, and it would lift its head up and you'd hold a cow up by his nose; he'd lift his head.

You had a *glass* bottle, which you'd push beyond their teeth to give them their medicine. You had to know what you were doing!

The big flagons were full of cider or ale for the men working, those doing a lot of scythe working. The Boss would go in, so unknown to him, and the men, we'd nip across and have a swig! This was on any farm. Most of them had young lads and I would go up and play. We weren't supposed to be drinking cider, but it was always made on the farms when I was a boy.

---

71 Became 'The Hardware of Combe Martin Ltd', a business which closed in 2012.
72 'Saint Peter ad Vincula' is St Peter in Chains.
73 From the village centre to Church Corner in Combe Martin is 2.3 miles.

'HENTON HILL', THE VILLAGE AND NEARBY

St Peter's, Combe Martin c.1900s. Pictorial Stationery Co.

Henry L'Argent: Twiss, Draper, Milliner, Newsagent Cc.1890s.

Beaumont's Stores c.1940s.

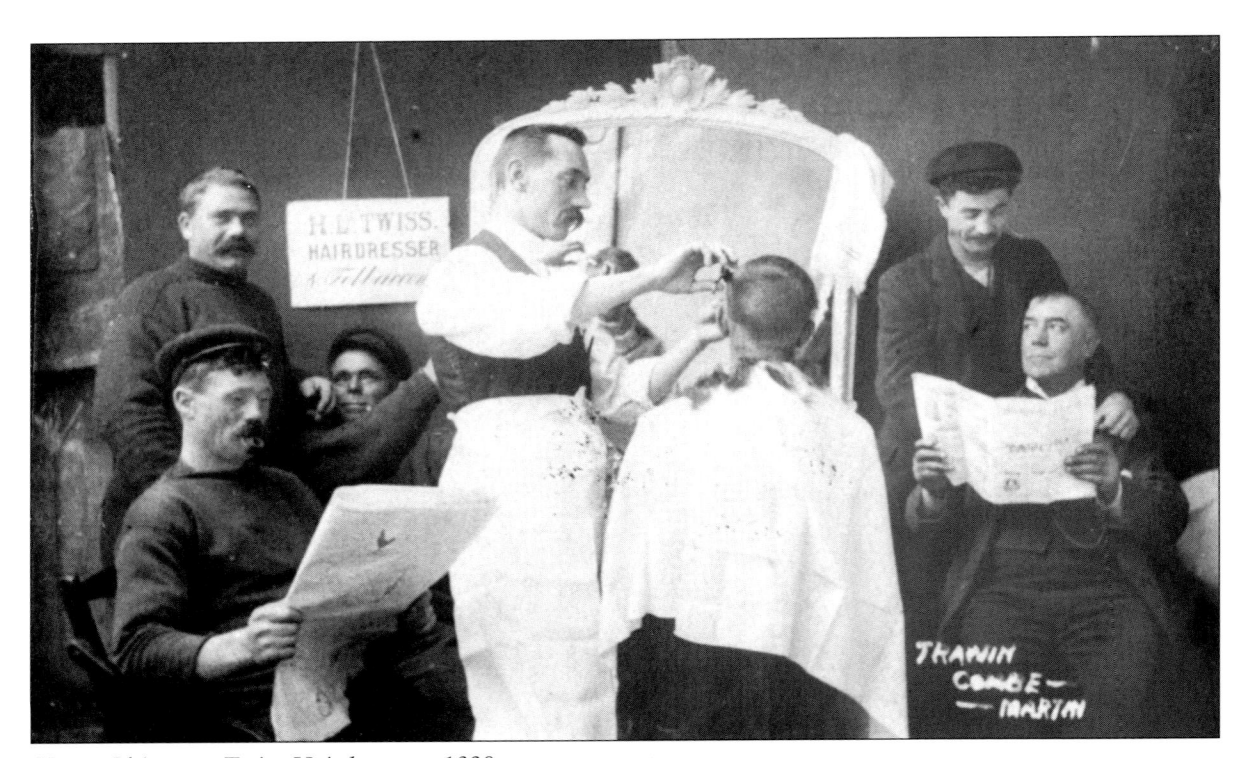

Henry L'Argent: Twiss Hairdresser c.1890s. Trawin, Combe Martin

'HENTON HILL', THE VILLAGE AND NEARBY

Donkeys at Watermouth c.1904.   Pictorial Picture Co. © Photograph from the Tom Bartlett Collection, EX34 9SE

One of the farms I used to play on was Hole Farm [Berrynarbor]. The farmer was Mr Jim Ley and he had three boys: Fred, Reg and John. Fred was the eldest, then Reg, then John. Reg lives in Ilfracombe. The older two went to Berrynarbor School, John may have done but I don't remember. He's now living in Barnstaple.

Will Bray, Taylor Bray, we called him. He used to measure you up, make a part, and bring it to you to try on. He lived where the pet shop is [Pets' Pantry], opposite the Post Office.'

That's Mrs Betsy Leworthy [4th from left in the photograph above]. She'd gone on before *I* was alive, but her husband Alf was a gardener at the Castle [Watermouth]. She used to keep about eight donkeys. She'd give the holidaymakers rides around the village and she used to go down to the pier, Ilfracombe, with them too.

There weren't no cattle lorries then. There and back it's about eight miles, but they didn't bother in them days about walking, but it's a long way to take donkeys without transport, I can tell you. She had two fields, behind North Lee; one was called 'Betsy's field'. I think the fields have grown over now and it's woodland.

She lived at Manor Cottage [Berrynarbor]. Betsy and Alf had two daughters: Annie and Florrie and a son, Alfie.

Annie never married; she was a real 'old maid'.[74] She was 'lively'; she didn't go dancing; she'd keep herself to herself, but she'd tell you off! I used to go scrumping[75] in her garden for apples. Not only me, but *others as well*! Their garden included the children's playground by the side of the Manor Hall.

Alfie, lived next to me, on the Haggington Hill, when I was first married. Alfie and Vera had two sons, Eric and Colin. We used to sit together, bring our chairs outside, by the roadside and sit opposite the stile. We used to have a good laugh... clean jokes... but he was a character! He used to drive a steam-roller for the council. He worked with my father.'

◇ ◇ ◇

---

74 An 'old maid' was a common term for a single woman, a spinster.
75 The word 'scrumpy: a rough dry cider brewed esp in the West Country' is derived from the verb, to scrump, often used when stealing apples 'from an orchard or garden.'

Chapter 4

First Employment and Life in the '30s

Educational Acts raised the school-leaving age from twelve to fourteen in 1921, to fifteen in 1944 and sixteen in 1973, and, therefore, Ron's formal education was over by the time he was fourteen, in the summer of 1934.

Career opportunities for any child in the 30s were limited and variety was lacking, particularly for those in rural communities, but Ron knew what he wanted to do: 'I always wanted to work on a farm.'

Formal education, for many of today's children, begins at primary school, usually at five, continues through secondary school and on to a college or university. Further or higher education can mean that students are in their twenties before they begin their first paid employment.

His first 'job' was to help Jack Geen, his stepfather, with road care and repair. This was his first 'employment' but he did not receive a weekly wage.

Jack was born during Queen Victoria's reign, 1837-1901. Road surfaces and edges were attended to by 'Lengthmen', ostensibly, a Victorian institution; they were responsible for between three and six miles of road. A Victorian map of the village mentions an 'Old Quarry' near the 'Limekiln' in 'Bament's Wood'. Their repair material was sourced from here.

This 'institution' has returned to many parishes; Berrynarbor is one of many up and down the country that employs a 'Parish Lengthman'. Their duties include road surface improvement and litter and drainage clearance; however, Ron believes that the roadsides were 'far tidier than they are today!'

'Jack had to tender for the contract every two or three years. He had the contract for several years to clear and repair the roads. Jack was my Boss, but he used to have a foreman: Fred Norman, I think. He'd come round and check. He'd be on his motorbike.

When I was working on the roads it was Jack, Joe Huxtable and me. After I went to the farm, when I was nearly sixteen, Jack worked for the council with Alfie Leworthy and Frank Melhuish.

Joe used to come from Ilfracombe. He'd come rain or shine. He lived up at Slade, but he only had a bicycle.[76] Jack paid *him*, but I had to *earn* my keep. My stepfather would give me some pennies at the weekends. I'd get 'jelly babies' or 'wine gums' from the Stores.

We left at 8.00 a.m. in the morning taking our sandwiches; if it was wet, we sat in somebody's shed to eat them. We used to work all around: the Sterridge Valley, Smythen Hill and Cross Park; we'd also look after Haggington Hill, past Woolscott Farm and up to Iron Letters Cross.[77]

If Jack had to go elsewhere, he'd take me in the mornings to where we were working: on our bicycles or we'd walk. Then he'd leave me and he'd say "You start here." He'd make a mark on the road or hedge and tell me where I had to finish that day. He wouldn't overwork me.

If it were frosty, we'd look where the frost hadn't been when we tidied up the roads. We'd do under the trees and that.

If it was really wet, we used to go round the roads with special canes, like the chimney sweeps use, and we'd unchoke the gutters and flush the water down. There are more houses around now and less space for the water to run.

The hedges were kept cut back by their owners. Probably, they were cut once a year, maybe more. We had to cut the banks on the roadsides; we'd use a pairing hook, a half-rounded hook with a short handle; they were always cut knee high. After we'd used the hook, we could use an old-fashioned shovel, sort of heart-shaped, to cut back the bank too.

We used a maddock[78] to pull out or cut back the weeds, the nettles and that. No weed killers were used then. We used a staff-hook with a long handle to take out a long branch, if it was growing out up high.

We used to leave our shovels and maddocks under the hedges, over in the fields. They'd still be

---

76 It is more than five miles from this part of Ilfracombe to Berrynarbor: the terrain is hilly.
77 This junction forms part of the parish boundary. Ron remmebres the actual 'iron letters'.
78 Devon dialect for 'mattock', a type of large pick that has one blade shaped like an adze.

FIRST EMPLOYMENT AND LIFE IN THE '30S

there in the morning. You could leave them there for several days and they'd still be where you left them. If you were near a farmer's cart shed, you could put them in there.

We used a broom; everything was swept up. It was very tidy. Roadside rubbish, such as the leaves, cuttings from the hedges and verges were piled up in rows, *small piles* and left in various places. On certain days, these were collected and taken away by a horse-drawn wooden farm butt by Len Dummett, who was then working for Claude Richards at Hammonds [Farm].

You'd take the rubbish to a farmer's field: it was mainly grass and weeds, but you'd ask the farmer and you'd fill a pit, a hole in a particular field. Nothing was wasted; most farms had holes or pits to fill, or we'd take it up to Bament's or the woods in the Sterridge.

The roads were repaired with stones dug from the quarry. Its entrance was just above the 'Napps' entrance. My father and I would go up there. You can't see it now; it's all overgrown.

We had to make a hole to put the dynamite powder in to split the rock. It was *hard* stone.[79] He'd put the bar iron, which was about one inch square [25mms], into a rock. The iron you started the hole with was the one you had to finish it with. It was a straight bar, pointed and sharp at the end.

We'd put a sack on the rock and I'd sit on the sack for a couple of hours. It was always my job to sit and turn the bar. It had to be turned after *every* time he hit the bar with his hammer. I'd have to hold it *very* steady.

We'd put water in the hole and we'd put grass on the ground around the bar to stop the water flying out. The water would soften the stone and when the hole was deep enough the dynamite went into the hole.

Then we'd leave the site. There weren't many cars, but there were buses. So we'd go on along the main road: one of us walked towards Combe Martin and stand there; and one of us walked towards Ilfracombe and hold up any bus until the explosion had happened.

The rocks had to be smashed into smaller pieces so we could lift them. We used a different iron bar, about four foot long [120cms] to prise the rocks apart. This one was bent at the end to prise them apart. They'd be big pieces of rock! It was hard work, especially for me as a boy.

Building Chaloner's Road, Braunton - 1930. R.A.P. Co. Ltd., London.
©Photograph from the Tom Bartlett Collection, EX34 9SE

79 See Appendices

'We'd break up these rocks with hammers to make them smaller, so they could be loaded onto a horse-drawn farm butt. My father and I didn't load them. My Uncle Dan used to send a man to collect them and then they were taken to the depots around the village.

The long, straight lay-by, by the wall of Mill Park, hasn't always been a lay-by; it was one of perhaps ten stone depots. The one nearest to the saw mill's quarry was at Mill Park. We would crack the big stones into smaller pieces, chippings, at the depots.

Me and me father would go to all of the depots and spend days chipping at these stones to make them smaller, so they could be picked up with the forks. When we chipped at the stone we wore gauze glasses and used 'ammers: that would be another couple of days work. The chippings weren't as small as they are today; they'd be about cup size.

The chippings were loaded onto a horse-drawn wooden farm butt with special stone forks. They had about six prongs, wide enough apart so the stones wouldn't drop through and they were curved at the ends, so the stones wouldn't drop off!

To empty the stones from the butt, a man would stand on the shafts behind the back of the horse, with his back to the horse's backside. He'd take off the tailboard and tip the butt, so the stones would go where they were wanted. Earth was added and then water from a horse-drawn water cart.

The steamroller was the council's; it usually came from Braunton and it rolled the mix onto the roads. It was a hard job for the horse to walk on the loose rough stones; they couldn't grip. After the roller had been used it was all right.

The council didn't have their own horses; they had to speak to the farmers and borrow theirs. It was my step-father's job to find people to do it.

Road repair and steamroller.

The roads were always rougher than they are now because the surface was easier for the horses. It was happy days working on the roads. We used to have time for a chat, mostly with the farmers. There wasn't the rushing around like there is today.

Caen Street, Braunton c.1953. E.A. Sweetman, Tunbridge Wells

FIRST EMPLOYMENT AND LIFE IN THE '30S

'Old Cottages in Braunton', Saunton Road c.1904. J. Valentine
Note the hayrick with its 'thatch' on the left, and the road condition.

Cross Tree, Braunton c.1904. W.H.Smith. 'Kingsway'
The 'Cross Tree' was felled on 7 February 1935 to allow the Exeter Road to come through. A plaque and street sign commemorate the location of this old oak tree.

LIFE IN THE 30s

Memories of those farmers illustrate the type of community Ron knew as a teenager and a young man. Their social entertainment was like the children's toys, manmade. In addition to religious commitments, events occurred in homes and establishments around the village.

'There was Bob Lancey at Orchard Farm, Will Lerwell – Farmer Bill – he was at Lower Rowes; Jack Huxtable was at Cockhill; Jim Bowden had Higher Rows; Jack Street lived opposite the tap house in the Sterridge; he had a *big* garden behind planted up with veg. Will Bowden was at South Lee and then there was Dan Toms, my uncle, at Middle Lee. Will Huxtable was at North Lee; he owned the land where the playing field is and he had quite a lot of ground 'over the top': about 20 acres off Ridge Hill.[80]

The villagers drove their market carts once or twice a week to Ilfracombe and Barnstaple. There were brakes on the market carts. There was a handle, attached to an arm, then to rubber blocks on the wheels of the market cart. You could pull up the lever and the brakes would go on both sides.

When you went to market, Barnstaple or Ilfracombe, two of you would sit, side by side; the driver was always on the right-hand side. Barnstaple Market was Tuesdays and Fridays for vegetables. Friday was the day for the sale of cattle and sheep in the Cattle Market.

The carts and farm butts didn't have any brakes, so going downhill, most farmers used a wheel drug on steep hills. Lester Bowden who had Sloley *had* to use a metal drug. You needed one to get down that steep hill towards *'is* farm. You would put them on the ground at the top of the hill, and as the horse went forward with a heavy load, the cart wheel or wheel of the butt would go into the drug and slide more slowly down the hill.

The drugs were one flat thick piece of iron between two very small wheels. It would be the left-hand wheel usually to go into the drug; it wasn't part of the cart or a farm butt and they were more rough and ready than the coach drugs. At the bottom you'd unload the cart, put the drug in to the cart or butt and it would be there for you next time. A horse would do 'is bit too in holding it back; they'd been so used to it.'

'There were farmers on Castle Hill too, but it wasn't known as Castle Hill in my day. It was always known as Pisspot Hill! Me stepfather's uncle lived up here and the story goes that one day a wife threw the 'pot' out of the window at her husband... Sounds a rude name but that's what it was!

If they hadn't got a milk round they'd take the milk into Ilfracombe. Norman Richards' father, Ivor, used to take two or three ten-gallon churns to Ilfracombe with his horse and trap in all weathers. He had Moule's on Castle Hill.

Hammonds Farm, past Croft Lee, was farmed by 'old' Claude Richards and before him, Ben Richards, father of Fred who had Home Barton. Ben was the first one I knew at Hammonds, after 'old Claude, his nephew, 'young' Claude Richards, took it on.

Derek Newton used to work for him pretty reg'lar. During the war, he drove the tractor on the farm; we had to plough up more land for the war effort. When he still had the dairy he had to help with this too.

When the milking machines came in, 'Young' Claude had his dairy at Dunchideock. Claude had his own bottles. The bottles were two pints, one pint and ½ pint and all had cardboard lids that sat just inside the top.

He brought the churns down, with the milk in, from the farm. He used to sleep there too and then he'd go up to the farm in the mornings; he was a single lad.

We didn't have refrigerators; we kept it cool by putting a jug of milk in cold water and covered it with a cloth. The cream and the butter were kept cool on the shelves inside the well in the garden. Most people had wells. I should think, most probably, there were five at Barton Farm.

When I went to Home Barton, there were three wells, but there was a man in the village, old William [Bill] Draper, and he'd come up to the farm and find water. He'd use a wooden, V-shaped stick, divining, they call it. I saw him do it on the farm and he'd dig for more wells. They were in different fields and the water was piped to the farm and to the other houses nearby. He did have a man to help him: Bill Dennis, a Combe Martin man, but he'd dig it by hand, mind you. He'd dig... ooh... ten feet down probably; he'd come across rock... well it was shale really.

Bill Draper was a hard working man, I can tell you. Him and his son-in-law, Jack, used to work in Lynton.[81] They knew the short cuts, but they'd leave about five on a Monday the morning, daylight or dark, wet or dry. I don't know what he did there, but he wasn't afraid of work. They'd stay the week and come home on Friday nights. He was a marvellous fellow.

---

80 The 'Berrynarbor' entry in the 1939 edition of *Kelly's Directory* listed 28 farms in this parish. Over the years, many have diversified or become committed totally to the West Country's tourist industry; however, Moule's Farm continues as a dedicated farm, one of a 'handful' in this parish.
81 Berrynarbor to Lynton, using the coastal route, is approximately 10 miles, 16 kilometres.

FIRST EMPLOYMENT AND LIFE IN THE '30S

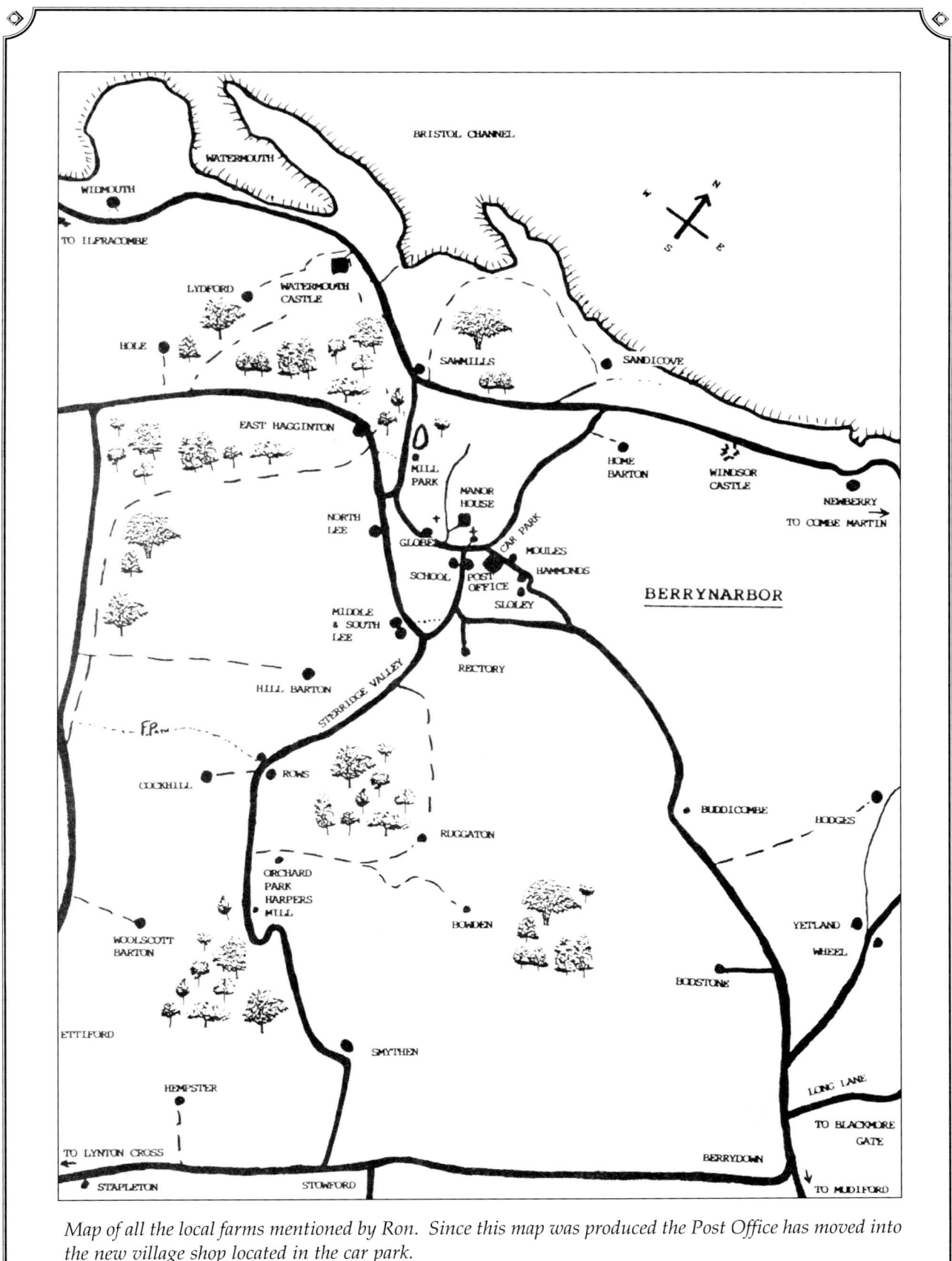

Map of all the local farms mentioned by Ron. Since this map was produced the Post Office has moved into the new village shop located in the car park.

He'd go out to work every day, even when he was in his 70s and on a Sunday afternoon he'd take his wife, Ellen, out in their donkey cart. There wasn't room for two in the cart, so he'd hold the side of the donkey's head, the head collar, and he'd run alongside! He sold the donkey to the owner of the Sandy Cove Hotel;[82] Mr Ratkin his name was.

The village people went to an indoor market, in Market Street, Ilfracombe, on Wednesdays and Saturdays; it's blocked off now. They used to take all their produce, buy things and stay for the day; it wouldn't take long to trot in by horse. They used to take chickens in too.

If they didn't sell something they would take it into Barnstaple on Fridays. They'd take their veg too; they always had plenty and generally it used to go like hot cakes. The older properties in the towns didn't have the gardens.

They didn't all go to the market, but most of them would go to the Cattle Market in Barnstaple. I believe it's one of the car parks now.

When I was in my teens about twenty of us joined the Young People's League, generally on a Wednesday. It was between 7.30 and 9.30pm and held in the Parish Rooms, but it was nothing to do with the church; it was like a youth club. There was always an older adult supervising, but anyone could join it. I can't remember anybody in particular. If the weather was rough we wouldn't all be there.

We had two Harvest Suppers, every October, when the chapel *was* a chapel.[83] We would have different dates so we wouldn't clash and we could go to the one at the chapel *and* at the church. We were all one; there were no arguments. If people were church members it didn't matter: they could and *would* go to the chapel supper as well.

The chapel's supper was held where they had the Sunday school: the bit on the right as you look at it. It's two houses now [Church House[84] and School House]. There was always enough food for everybody.

The church supper *was* in the Manor Hall. There wasn't always a kitchen at the Hall, so every lady used to bring something.

About Christmas-time, the Bible Class group and their wives or girlfriends had a Christmas meal, which was brought from the Rectory. It was taken to the Parish Rooms, for about 20-odd people. Servants from the Rectory used to help; they'd bring the food over in a wheelbarrow. Two or three would dish it out for us. It was a good night. It was a hot meal, even though it was wheeled over from the Rectory. We had turkey and all the trimmings and Christmas pudding.

I didn't care for Christmas pudding, but two or three lads used to see who could eat the most! The one who did was well known in the village: Leonard Dummett. He had ten brothers and sisters.

There was lemonade to drink, but it was tea and coffee mainly. No beer, well you wouldn't for a parson's do. We used to sing carols after our dinner.

Before I was old enough, my stepfather went to Bible Classes, at Orchard House. Men of fifty and sixty used to go too. There'd probably be about thirty of us in all. It was the Men's Bible Class, for the boys and men... no girls!

When I went to Home Barton, I was old enough to go too. I didn't go to the Young People's League then; it didn't run for very long. Me and young Brian Richards would go, on a Monday.

This was in the winter months, for about three or four months: on dark evenings, before and after Christmas. We were all busy in the summer; we were mainly farm workers.

The Reverend Churchill used to have his say and read some Bible verses and then we would have to read. Some boys didn't like reading aloud. I didn't mind so I would read theirs too.

We talked about religious things and had a pile of old leaflets called 'Ashore and Afloat'. They were connected with the sea and to do with the Bible as well. We all had a different one. They weren't new each week. The Reverend Churchill had collected them; I don't know where from.

At the end of the evening, he used to say, "Goodnight boys" and leave us to it. There was a nice fire and we'd sit there talking. The last one out would lock up and take the key to Ernest Richards.

Other evenings, the old men in the village would come home from work, eat their meal, a good cooked meal, have a wash and a shave and off they'd go to The Glob where they played games: cards, shove ha'penny and dominoes. It used to close about 10, 10.30pm.

---

82 Located on the Old Coast Road, this hotel overlooks the sea; it is in walking distance from the village.
83 Its foundation stone was laid on 'June 6th 1881'. Ron refers to it as the Congregational Church and his comment of 'We were all one' is supported by the meaning of Congregationalism, which is 'a system of Christian doctrines and ecclesiastical government in which each congregation is self-governing and maintains bonds of faith with similar local congregations.'
84 'By 1824...a school had been established in the former vestry room in the Church House adjoining and on the south of the churchyard. The rest of the Church House was used as the Poorhouse. The earliest reference then existing to this building was a deed of 1697.'

FIRST EMPLOYMENT AND LIFE IN THE '30S

Christmas at the Manor Hall. 'This was in the Manor Hall, before I was married. At the front, on the floor, is me and Noeleen, Fred Richards' youngest. He's behind her. On his left is his eldest, Vera; Violet Toms, my cousin, is next to her and last on the right. Ivy Richards is next to Fred [his right] and Ivy's sister Phyllis is to her right. Then its Dolly Dummett, Vera Dummett and Brenda Layton neé Richards [sister of Vera and Noeleen], is at the end of this row with Cheryl her daughter. Back row, from the left, its: Lorna Grove-Price neé Richards, Percy Thomas and Lily Richards: she was my school teacher. Next is Ivy Jones; she worked on the farm when Bob and Bett Richards worked it. She did the housework two or three times a week. Young Claude Richards and Muriel Richards are next, and then it's Bruce Stanbury or his brother Ken. Next is Heather Jones, daughter of Ivy, then its Miss Veale, [with the pearls], then Mrs Cooperthwaite. I think the last lady [with the hat] was the parson's wife, but it wasn't the Reverend Churchill.

There were Whist Drives, in the Manor Hall, generally on a Wednesday evening. They were weekly and very popular and had been going for *years*.

At Christmas time they had a *really* big one and there were prizes of turkeys, geese and other poultry. They were all plucked and set up ready for cooking; or perhaps they'd have a piece of pork. They were all given by the local farmers.

I never went before I was married and I didn't go after. My wife and I weren't card players.'

◇ ◇ ◇

Chapter 5

Farming Life

Beginnings...

*A*griculture is believed to be the world's oldest industry; once, soil was tilled with hand-held sticks or tree branches. Sticks became oxen-drawn ploughs that assisted for centuries; bovine became equine that had arrived in the 14th century and was the farmers' friend for six hundred years; however, international warfare, the First World War, 1914-18, created an urgent need for increased food production.

With war at the door, the proverbial saying of, 'Necessity is the mother of invention' became somewhat pertinent as it was acknowledged that mechanisation would benefit the hungry: horse and steam power were costly, laborious and labour intensive.

The mass-produced Fordson tractor[85] *arrived during this conflict; it captured, then retained, much of the market for many years. Fierce competition resulted: names such as David Brown, John Deere and Ferguson were applied to the 'mechanical horse' too and became familiar countryside sights as horse and steam gradually began to disappear from farms.*

Ron's childhood memories are of living, playing and helping out on farms. It is, perhaps, unsurprising, with this background and the agricultural dominance of his birthplace, that he grew up knowing that he wanted to earn his living from the land and follow his grandparents, uncle and stepfather, but horse power ran supreme for many years.

Whilst Ron was still 'just a youngster, on the Hill', Jack led by example; he was always willing to tackle any task to earn 'a bob or two.'

'He used to go to Braunton on his motorbike every morning to pick up his machinery and a mate. He'd built a shed in the garden for his bike!

He worked for a man, a contractor called Isaacs.[86]

They used to go round different farms with a coal-fired thresher, to thresh the corn. You had to have two men: one was the driver; Jack was the one to stoke the fires and keep the coal up to keep the engine going.

The thresher separated the corn from the straw: the stalks of the corn. You would only do it on a fine day, in the winter. You couldn't thresh when it was wet

It took a bit of manoeuvring to get the thresher around the corners at some farms, like Hammonds Farm; it was 'old' Claude's then and was the trickiest to get in to. They used metal 'spuds', to get into a small yard. They were good iron, V-shaped, made by the blacksmiths. They were used for the back wheels to skid off the wall, on tight corners. They didn't use machinery, diggers and such like to dig out the rock; they used the spud, but they weren't used everywhere. It had to be carried on the machine all the time.

The front wheels would work easy; they'd be all right, but the back wheels didn't turn as easily as the front ones. The front wheels were smaller, perhaps half the size. The driver could see the front wheels; he'd be up in a big cab.

A big steam coal-fired road locomotive would pull the thresher. Isaacs had three or four locomotives and threshers; they'd go to different farms, and it was the farmers' place to get the coal in before they came.

Threshing would take two or three days then; they were allowed to stay overnight on the farms and then they'd go on to other farms. They'd come to Home Barton when I was there.

Jack went up to mend the fences at Home Barton, so I went along to see how things were: to have a look. Fred Richards had a man leaving... Fred Wilcox.'

---

85 The brand name for a mass-produced range of all-purpose tractors and, as the name suggests, made, originally, by Henry Ford and Son between 1917 and 1920. They became the Ford Motor Company, but the 'Fordsons' continued until 1964. American manufacture ceased in 1928, moved to Southern Ireland in 1929 and then, eventually, to Dagenham, Essex.
86 Blacksmiths and wheelwrights worked from Isaac's Yard on the Wrafton Road in this village. The 'Yard' has been developed; Braunton School and Community College has a new hall and canteen, named the 'Isaac Hall'.

◆ FARMING LIFE ◆

'They're threshing corn and putting it on a rick. The man on the ground is collecting bits and putting it on a cart. The straw was taken to a barn'.

Fred Richards, the farmer, Stanley Harding, the farm's Horseman and the farmer's young children were also there. The farmer noticed the teenager, "I could do with a young lad like your boy."

Ron was asked if he would like to work here and the teenager agreed. Disparagingly perhaps, Jack added that he did not think he would stay long, but Ron worked for members of the Richards' family for fifty-three years.

When he was approaching his sixteenth birthday, 1932, he left home, taking his tin box of clothes, to live and work at Home Barton.[87] He began his new job on one of the four quarter days,[88] Lady Day, March 25th, which was a 'date for the payment of quarterly rates or dues' and when new staff were employed. He became one of the family and 'lived in'.

'I arrived just before 12; that's what was done then. I went to the back door of the farmhouse and knocked. The Boss came to the door and said, "You've come Ron – good..."

Obviously, I didn't know what my first job would be, but you had to do what you were told then. He pointed and said, "Go to that door there and take a broom and a fork. Go down to the bottom of the yard to *that* door and clean out."

I took the broom and fork, opened the other door and discovered there was a bull inside! I went and said to him, "There's a bull in there Boss!" "I know there is," he said, "but *he's* tied *up!*" I was shaking inside as I was doing it, but I did it!

The farmyard when I first went there was all

---

[87] For Ron, 'Barton' means a farm with 100 acres or more but, originally, it was 'a common name, usually OE *beret n, bær-t n* 'barley farm, outlying grange where corn is stored'. Kelly's Directory, 1939, stated that some farms were '150acres or over'. Home Barton had this description.
[88] June 24th: Midsummer Day, September 29th: Michaelmas Day and December 25th: Christmas Day. In addition, to the September fiscal event, it was the month when, on tenanted farms, an outgoing farmer would take his crops, which enabled the incoming tenant to prepare and plant his.

cobblestones. It was difficult to push the wooden wheelbarrows [see above] with their wooden wheels across the yard I can tell you!

When we were cleaning out the bull's shed, we'd put him out in the farmyard too and he'd wander around *and* I've seen them smash wooden gates and wheelbarrows!

They *could* be in with the cows in their shed, but they'd be tied to a good strong pole. He had to have a strong chain around his neck; they had some weight behind them and they had their horns. You had to watch yourself! There was a ring around the pole and the chain would be attached to this so the bull could move his head up and down.

We always kept one bull on the farm for our own purpose. Not every farm had a bull, so when it was mating time other cows were brought to Home Barton: from the Sterridge Valley, up at Higher Rows and Lower Rowes. The Devon[89] bulls could be nasty; you had to keep your eye out. The Devons are red in colour.

Our Devon bull was all right, but you had to keep an eye on him, particularly when he'd just served the cows. He was a bit wicked then; you'd taken away the cows! The Boss would leave you to take him back to the barn to chain him up!

We used to have the staddlestones too [see below] on the farm when I first went there. I suppose over the years they got broken. They were made of stones and cement, but were smooth on the outside so the rats couldn't climb up to eat the corn. They were about two to three feet high, [60-90cms]. We'd put poles across the top of four of them

Red Ruby Devon Cow

and the corn was put on top. They were cemented in and stayed there year round and were in the rick yard. In them days it was just for the ricks[91] and nothing else. It was a big open yard for corn and hay, but mainly for the corn. A few steps from the farm-yard, you'd be in the rick yard.

We had farm cats at Middle Lee and Home Barton, but all the farms would keep cats to get rid of the rats then. The Missus would go into the shippen[92] and she'd hear their kittens in the hay loft above, it would be my job to hold them up to her; it would be her decision which ones to keep, but we'd always keep the she cats because they were better for catching the rats.

With tom cats around they were *always* having kittens! The farm cats were outside, but they'd have their kittens in the hay lofts or anywhere warm.

They'd feed the rats to their young – no cat food then! If you put some scraps down, they'd come to

---

89 The Red Ruby Devon cows are prized for their good temperament, unlike the bulls, and for their marbled succulent meat.
90 Also known as mushroom stones; 'staddle' is an Old English word for 'stump'. Originally, these 'stumps' were made to support buildings: tithe barns and granaries.
91 'A large stack of hay, corn, peas etc., built in the open in a regular-shaped pile, especially one with a thatched top.'
92 Devon dialect: a milking parlour.

◇ FARMING LIFE ◇

the back door, but you wouldn't give them too much otherwise they wouldn't go catching! They wouldn't go far from the yard.

Years ago, there were rat catchers living in the village, but Ben Brooks lived nearby, in Hele. He'd come to the village and catch them. I was told about him. He'd come to the village to see his sister Ellen. She lived at Court Cottage [Birdswell Lane]. When he came to the village he'd make a bit of money on his way catching the rats from the houses. The last one I knew was Gordon Newton; he lived up Haggington, near to me when I was married.

On the farm, Home Barton, we had rat catchers employed by the council. They'd put down bait and the farmer would pay for the catcher. They'd have a round to do: for all the farms. You could catch them yourselves, when you were allowed to use the gin traps.[93] You used the same traps for the rats and rabbits.

A good dog, a terrier, would catch them too. If you were asked in the morning, "How are you?"

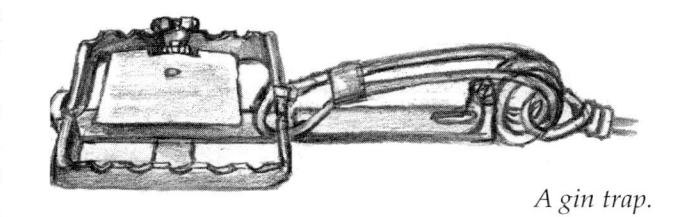

A gin trap.

you'd say, "Rough and ready, like a rat catcher's dog!"

'he was a good father and boss.'

The Boss and the Missus, Fred and Emma, had Vera, Brenda, Freda, Brian, Robert, Claude and Noeleen. 'Noel Maureen' was born on Christmas Day. She was about twelve months old when I went there, so ten of us sat down three times a day.

Breakfast, about 7.00am was usually fried. We had eggs, bacon, fried mashed potatoes, sausages and fried bread. Lunch was about 10.00am and often

Emma, Noeleen, and one of her brothers in the yard, preparing a bullock for a Young Farmers' show. The bull's 'pen' is behind them.

---

93 Gin traps had metal jaws that snapped shut and caught or maimed rats and rabbits, but could also trap other unsuspecting victims such as household pets, foxes, birds and humans. Originally, these were made by local blacksmiths, but then they were mass-produced and used until they were banned from legal use in 1958.

'The Missus': Emma with Noeleen, her youngest.

There was no use arguing with their father; he was stern. If he told you to do something, you *had* to do it, but he was a good father and boss.

They were very good to me, like parents. The Missus would always give me half-a-crown[94] for my birthday, when I was living in; that was a lot of money in them days.'

As I was living in, I used to go for a walk sometimes...not very far. Noeleen was only young, but she'd come with me. She'd look at the flowers and point and I'd pick them for her. She would give the flowers to her mother; her mother thought the world of them.

Wherever I was in the yard, she'd follow me. The others were at school and the Missus would shout, "Ron... Noeleen's coming." She'd follow me around the yard and she'd help to collect the eggs.

'the bigger the hen the better.'

We had about forty to fifty laying hens. A horse would pull the chicken arc or coop out to the field; it was arched and on wheels. They'd be let out and they'd eat the corn scraps and lay their eggs in the arc, usually, and then come back out. Sometimes they would go into the hedges and around the yard. The arc could be left out in the fields for days.

A broody hen would sit off and on her eggs, in the coop. Once the eggs had hatched, the chicks would hang around their mother and she'd look after them.

Before the incubators were about they used the mother hens; they'd put geese, ducks or turkey eggs under a hen. You wouldn't mix 'em. You could only put four goose eggs under and about six turkey eggs; goose eggs are the biggest, but it would depend on the size of the hen. When the hen sits down and spreads her wings you'd be surprised at the space they'd cover: the bigger the hen the better!

We'd wet the eggs and they would sit on them for several weeks and turn them. We'd give them food and drink... and we'd check on 'em.

'There was tractors in them days; farmers had their own, but they weren't as big as they are today. They were the Fordsons. I don't know of any round here *before* the war; Home Barton had its first during the war [WWII], but there were mainly horses round here then.

Stanley Harding, George's son, helped me when I first went to Barton Farm. *He* was important because he *was* the Horseman. He looked after the team; 'Madam and Darling' were the team when I first went there.

boiled eggs and homemade bread and butter. Dinner would be about 1.00am; the Boss would carve large joints of meat and everybody helped themselves from the dishes of vegetables that were grown on the farm and in the garden. After we'd done the afternoon's milking we'd have tea, around 5.30pm. It was sandwiches and cakes. All meals were washed down and finished with a cup of tea; the milk and cream came from our cows.

I used to lift Noeleen on to the bench. She'd sit by me and want *my* food and I'd have to take some of hers!'

Noeleen's still alive, but the others have all gone on now. Noeleen lives in Birmingham.

The girls would help their mother in the house, like stripping the walls and papering, when they were big enough. They didn't help in the fields because we had the farm hands.

---

94 'half-a-crown' is two shillings and six pence or 12.5 pence in today's money.

FARMING LIFE

Home Barton Farm and two horses.

Typical milking equipment for Ron: a stool and bucket.

He helped me a lot, 'showed me the ropes' so to speak, 'cos the Boss was often away from the farm on his committees. His father, Ben, had been on committees.

Fred was on all sorts of committees: the school, the church, the Manor Hall and the Parish Council... He was on the War Agricultural Committee too.

Stan married a Berrynarbor girl and they lived at Croft Lee, but he used to walk to work over the fields. *His* first job in the morning *was* feeding the horses, but while they were feeding he'd come across the yard to the shippen to help me milk the cows.

We had forty to fifty milking cows and they were all hand-milked. We'd collect the milk from the cow in a milk bucket. You'd collect it all from one cow and then you'd pour it in the churn, through the strainer at the top.

About three of us would do the work and we'd have so many each. It'd be Stan, me, the Boss if he was there, or their eldest son, Brian. Their elder boys could be about nine or ten, but if they were big enough, they had to learn to milk. Everybody that *could* help *would* help with the morning's milking.

The cows would be chained and we'd sit down on a small three-legged stool... wooden, to milk, but we had metal milking buckets. You couldn't use a wooden bucket because the milk had to be clean; it would stick to wood. We didn't wear posh coats or hats; we'd wash our hands and if we had a cap on, we'd turn it round so that the peak wouldn't stick into the cow and we'd rest our head on them.

We'd take our milk to Combe Martin to sell. This was one of their daily rounds, but we just had the morning's delivery. If you didn't sell it all, you'd scald some of it to make the cream. You could also give it to the pigs: mix it with their barley meal, especially if they had little ones.

On their way to school in the morning, the older Richards children would deliver some milk along Barton Lane; they'd drop it off to some people on their way down: only about five or six houses then. When their eldest boy Brian learned to drive, he would deliver it. They all did when they were old enough to drive.

When the morning milking was finished, Stan would go back to the stable and brush the horses down, put their harnesses on and take them out. He would put the neck collar on, which was soft and padded and then the ames with the metal crooks. They'd be fixed over the collar sockets that would take the chains.

The chains would be each side of the horse to take the implements. There'd be a wooden draught, before we had the iron ones, between the horse and the chains, to keep the space. The chains were long: they had to be if they were between the implement and the neck collar.

If they were pulling a butt they'd have a short 'tug chain' and a collar on too. The tug chains had to be kept hanging in the stable, so they were ready.

Only two would milk in the afternoon; the Boss would do it if he was home and somebody else would help *him*. The cows knew you. If you didn't handle them right, they'd kick you and if you lost milk down the drain, you'd get a black look from the Boss. He was a good boss though and so was his wife.

The Boss could milk a certain cow and she wouldn't move for him. If she did move, he'd speak to her firmly. She wouldn't kick but she'd shudder. If anybody else had to milk her, we'd have to tie her back legs together!

The churns were in the milking shed and when one was full you'd get another. It would be put into two or more 10-gallon churns, with taps on and then taken round Combe Martin and Berrynarbor.

From the left: Bob, Vera and Brian and the delivery van.

Fred and Emma had a van[95] for delivering the milk around Combe Martin and Berry. We had a measure to scoop out the milk or you could hold a container or jug under the taps.

Vera and Brenda were their oldest children, but Brian was the oldest boy.[96] The oldest ones who could drive would help deliver: around the village and Combe Martin. I used to help them; I wouldn't drive but I'd take the bottles to the houses.

The cows were chained up for milking. You'd pull hay down, from the loft, in the winter, and put it in the rack above their trough, which was for their mangels,[97] cabbages or cow cake. They had the grass when they were outside in the summer and they'd be back out in the fields after milking, in the morning and the evening.

They'd get cow cake all year round when you were milking. It kept them quiet and it would bring on the milk. Some would be quiet; others would kick frequently. Often they'd knock each other with their horns, to get to *their* place.

They were mainly the Devons, but we had a couple of Jerseys or Guernseys to give colour to the milk...more yellow. They were allowed to mate with the Devons so that all the milk was creamy. The Reverend Churchill had Jerseys and Guernseys too.

I used to fetch cream from the Rectory, and other farms including Hill Barton. It was sold to the villagers and it was sent by post in special ¼ lb or ½ lb tins, [113g or 226g]. People came here on holiday and sent it home to their parents.

The afternoon's milk would be put in the pan; it would be fresh and warm straight from the cow, so it would be left to settle overnight. In the morning it would be heated up carefully. You had to keep your eye on it. You'd let it rise just to the boil and then take it off the heat. You couldn't let it get any hotter because the pan would break.

It would be put back in the dairy on cold stone slabs and by morning it would be cooled off, so the milk would be scalded and skimmed; it was skimmed because you'd skim the cream off the top: could be with your hand! It wasn't hygienic, but nobody ever died from doing this! You could use a proper little flat scoop too. You'd scoop off the cream and put it into a cup or something.

This was clotted cream, but we didn't call it 'clotted cream' then. It was just real 'Devonshire cream' to us.

I don't think milk is as fresh today as it was when I was working: a morning's milking was delivered that morning, by 7.00 or 7.30am. Today it's pooled; it's collected from all the farms and taken to processing plants.

The afternoon's milking was left in churns and delivered the next morning. People weren't fussy if it was the morning's milk or the afternoon's, but some was left as 'new' and some was scalded for skimmed milk. If it was skimmed or 'scalded' milk it was, '3 ha'pence", [three half-pennies, just over 1p today].

The milk lorries came in later. After Fred had retired, Bob, his son, took over and he took on milking machines and the lorries would come with ten-gallon churns. They would come round and collect our churns and from other farms, and give us empty ones. At Dunchideock, outside there's a place to put the churns; it was easier for some farmers to put their churns *there*. We have the milk tankers now.[98]

---

95 Unhesitatingly, Ron stated that this was 'a Bean'. Bean Cars Ltd of Tipton, Worcester, was an offshoot of A. Harper & Sons Ltd, founded in 1901. Commercial vehicles were produced during the 1920s, but the company went into liquidation in 1931.
96 One of the School Registers records the names and birth dates of the Richards' children:
'Vera' '14.12.1914', 'Brenda May' '31.7.1916', 'Freda Annie' '26.4. 1918', 'Herbert Brian' '24. 7. 1920',
'Robert Benjamin' '16.8.1922', 'Frederick Claude' '16.11.1925', 'Noel Maureen' '25.12.1932'.
97 'Mangelwurzel or mangoldwurzel, a Eurasian variety of the beet plant, *Beta vulgaris*, cultivated as a cattle food, having a large yellowish root.'
98 Currently, milk tankers can take up to 30,000 litres of milk.

FARMING LIFE

'seasonal assignments...'

Most 'onlookers', those of us who drive or walk past the fields full of 'something' and are, generally, uninformed as to the agricultural calendar, appreciate that our climate and weather are dictators. We know that our four seasons affect what is undertaken and when the 'something' is grown, as we do not expect to see haymaking or a field filled with corn in December.

Whether to sow or not, for example, has never depended upon forecasting. Mother Earth and animal behaviour have been watched and used for centuries and the farming community here continued this process, even when the media and science arrived.

In 1923, when he was still a schoolboy, daily radio bulletins began and were presented by the BBC in collaboration with what was then the British Meteorological Office, now the Met Office. Transmission of television charts occurred from 1936, but ceased due to the closure of the BBC during World War II, but in 1954, two Forecast Officers job-shared to present daily reports and forecasts with charts; however, Ron's workplace was excluded.

'As the crow flies', there are around 23 miles across the Bristol Channel between the towns of Ilfracombe, North Devon and Swansea in South Wales. Unfortunately, because of this proximity, Berrynarbor, a few miles east of Ilfracombe, received BBC Wales from across the water; Welsh Language programmes and weather forecasts continued to be received until the late 1980s.

'There was a time of year for everything on the farm. We didn't have weather forecasts then, but we *used* the weather. My Boss could *tell* what the weather was going to be, others could too. He used to go out first thing in the morning and he'd look about.

Fred was a farmer's son; his father, Ben Richards, had farmed Hammonds. Hammonds and Home Barton's land meets at the top of a field. Fred, 'Old' Claude and Arch Richards were the sons and there was one daughter, Audrey. Arch Richards had Seven Ash Farm and his son still farms it today.

Years ago, we had winters and summers but if it was a wet day, we'd say, "When the rain is hard the rain is best." It was a day of rest; it wasn't *really*, but we also said that, "It was a day for the King," meaning that you didn't do so much. Something else that's been said here for years is that, "If you can see Wales and their lights shining, it's going to rain."

I was told, by Alfred Sloley, that there was a farmer, past Goosewell and up towards West Henton Farm, who couldn't see the sea from his farm as it's in a dip. He'd get on his pony and he'd go to where the golf links[99] are now and he'd look out to sea. He'd come back to his men and say, "We won't get much done outside today, the sea's full of water!" What he meant was that the sea was high and we'd get rain and he was usually right!

Another story from round here is that there was a farmer and his son who couldn't do much on the farm for a couple of days; on the third day it was *still* raining. The son said, "It's raining again father." The father replied, "You don't get two days alike boy! It's raining one day and wet the next!"

Autumn is synonymous with the end of the growing cycle, but it is the beginning of the farming calendar too.

Harvesting in 'Nearby' Knowle, C.1930, and a clear illustration of 'steep fields' and 'tall' crops.

99 Ilfracombe Golf Club

Hartnoll's Rick, Braunton, 1909. 'Threshing and reed combing with an Isaac's reed comber. The wheat stalks were cut by scythe or reaper, which meant minimum damage.'

Centuries ago, this was the season that produced the major part of a family's income, and, therefore, it was also the time for thanksgiving: by the landowners and their labourers. 'Harvests were a communal affair; farmers helped each other. Their harvest was completed and they could go to the Fair, in Barnstaple, in September.' This was an opportunity to relax and socialise after long hours of manual labour in the fields.

Harvest Festival offerings in the Congregational Chapel.

Pre-Henry VIII and his break from the Catholic Church, Harvest Festivals were celebrated at the beginning of the harvesting season, on 1st August, Lammas Day, meaning loaf-mass. This was when bread, made from the newly-harvested corn, was distributed at the Eucharist, the Holy Communion service.

Michaelmas Day, 29th September, is another one of our quarter days. In addition to it being another fiscal event, it was the time when, on tenanted farms, an outgoing farmer would take his crops, which enabled the incoming tenant to prepare and plant his.

Autumn fairs began as Harvest Fairs, these, the Festivals and Suppers are associated with the months of September and October. The familiar Harvest Festival services of today began in 1843, in Cornwall. Traditionally, churches nationwide are decorated with items of local produce, such as the recently cut corn or wheat and the harvested, the 'gathered...ripened crop', of fruits and vegetables.

'I think the Fair was September or October.'

'All your seed, corn and cow cake was *delivered* by delivery men; *they wouldn't* take *payment!* Farmers,

FARMING LIFE

Barnstaple High Street, 1920s. Shows this town as it looked when Ron was a boy.

Old Barum Fair, 1907.

W.S. Wood, Barnstaple
© Photograph from the Tom Bartlett Collection EX34 9SE

Barum Fair (from the air). Surrounding its location is: Castle Green and Mound to the right of the road; Rolle Quay bridge crosses the river. The train has left Barnstaple station and is heading towards Ilfracombe station, which closed in 1970.

most of them, would pay their bills once or twice a year at the Barnstaple Fair.[100] They'd pay their bills in the morning – and then go around the merchants, generally in the High Street at different offices; then they'd go to the Fair and have a good time... drinking and that.

A farmer and his wife would go into Barnstaple and he'd stay with his cattle or sheep until they were sold and his wife would go to the Pannier Market. The Pannier Market, as I can remember, was the same days as the Cattle Market: Tuesdays and Fridays, but Friday was the main day for cattle and sheep.

Barum Fair, 1908, the Sheep Fair. W.S. Wood, Barnstaple
© Photograph from the Tom Bartlett Collection EX34 9SE

Some farmers would bring back any unsold stock but if they didn't want to there was always somebody, the drovers,[101] willing to earn a bob or two. It wasn't a stated price; it would be agreed. It was a long way back to Berrynarbor *and* they'd have to get back to Barnstaple.

Often as not, they'd live near the Cattle Market. They'd have a bike and a good dog; they wouldn't be the youngsters. In them days, it wasn't difficult to get anybody to do extra: no problem at all.

You could pay 6d [2.5p] for a fairground ride on the horses, so you could do a lot with a couple of pounds at the Fair. I think the Fair was in September or October. I used to go as a boy, but there wasn't a carnival or a procession, it was just the Fair. It was a day out for children. We'd go in our horse and carts, on the Southern Nationals, the buses, or if somebody had a car they'd take us.

After I was married, I used to take my young children. Anyone could go.

'Arran Banners were big round potatoes'

We'd grow more of the maincrop potatoes than the earlies. They'd be dug up before the winter set in, about September or October. When it was time for the potatoes to be dug, we'd use the banking plough again, but this time with two horses, so the plough would split the row; it wouldn't damage them. It would dig deep under the potatoes and all the potatoes would show and drop each side. We'd walk. The only time we wouldn't walk would be sitting mowing or riding on a binder, or working the grass fit for hay. In later years, we'd use these potato spinners at the back of a tractor.

In the potato fields, after they were dug, some would be left and ones would be missed, but the pigs would find them. We had to watch them because if they got into another field, they would try and root up the grass, but the rings would stop them!

The farm pigs would have rings put through their noses when they were piglets: to stop them rooting up. The farmers would do this theirselves. They'd stick it into their snout; it probably hurt a bit, for a day or two. It's probably like a woman having her ears pierced!

We bagged them up into 1¼ cwt[102] sacks and two men picked up the sacks with what we called a granny stick; it would help to lift these on to the horse cart. It would be any stick from the wood, about three to four inches thick, so it was strong enough to lift the sacks; it would be bent in the middle.

One man would put his right hand to the mouth of the sack and one would use his left. They'd hold the ends of the stick and push it under the bottom of the sack to lift it on to the carts.

There'd probably be about eight to ten bags on a cart. The potatoes used to be taken to the barn and tipped out on the barn floor. This was only done on dry days. We tipped them through a little door halfway up the barn wall, but the varieties were kept separate.

In them days we had: Field Marshalls, Home Guards, Great Scot, Arran Banners, Dr McIntosh, King Edwards, Maris Pipers and Kerr's Pinks. Arran Banners were big round potatoes, a good cropper but too big really.

We'd use the hay cart for delivering the potatoes. The carts, farm butts and machinery didn't have any brakes, so you had to get used to using the long pole.

---

100 Barnstaple Fair is believed to have been founded by Alfred the Great's grandson, King Athelstan, who ruled between 925 and 939AD, and, therefore, it has the reputation of being one of the oldest in the country. It was a week-long affair, but is four days now, commencing on the Wednesday preceding the 20th September.
101 Usually, men, 'whose occupation (was) the driving of sheep or cattle, especially to and from market.'
102 A cwt, or hundredweight, is equal to 112 pounds or 50.80235 kilograms.

The long pole was a long strong stick cut from the wood in a hedge. You'd only have a long pole if you were using two or three horses. The pole could be attached to the mowing machine or even the binder. It would go between the horses from the machinery.

The carts had wooden rails on each side, but they were open-ended: back and front. There was ironwork, the stays, to keep the sides up. The pole was on the outside of the rails and it would be rubbing on the side of the wheel but not touching the road. It was wedged, towards the back part of the cart, was as long as the cart and tied with cord or rope to the ironwork, but it didn't touch the horses. It used to do the trick, but you couldn't pull it too tight; you had to let the wheel go round. The wheels had to be good. When you had a heavy load it had to be there all the time. If you were carrying hay, that wasn't heavy and we didn't need the pole.

We'd use a pole if we were going from Barton Farm down to Combe Martin. *We* had to deliver the potatoes to the market gardeners, to their shops, or the fish and chip shop, the Black and White, by the seaside. When you took the horse and cart with eight sacks of potatoes, about 1¼ cwt each, they were *heavy* and it was downhill all the way!

A lot of market gardeners had shops and if they didn't have enough potatoes they'd come to Home Barton and other farms.

On a wet day we could deliver ½ ton for one shop. We had to lift the sacks of potatoes; two of us would put them on to the cart. No use grumbling in them days; you had to do what you were told!

Sometimes they'd be delivered to the shops in Combe Martin and sometimes they'd be collected by the people in the village. Usually, when we were delivering, we'd put eight sacks on 'cos that would be ½ ton; that would be enough, but you could have up to twelve sacks on the cart if you were going downhill to Combe Martin.

We'd deliver the big potatoes to the Black and White. To take them in to the shop, you'd put the sacks to the tail end of the cart and you'd put your behind to the back and hold the sack on your back with your hands underneath and carry it in. This would be a wet day job.

All the chips were cut by hand! It would be somebody's job to stand there and peel them! If they were *really* big they'd often be hollow in the middle and wouldn't be any good for chips: no good at all... They'd be taken back and given to the bullocks.

'We'd do this with the turnips, mangels and the potatoes'

'When the corn had grown and been cut, you'd lift the corn roots out then you'd harrow it all over before you sowed another crop. You'd leave the roots to dry out for a few days in the fine weather. We used to have it then: *week after week*.

Once they were all dry you'd go into the field with a horse rake, the same one we'd use for the hay, collect them all up in rows and then we'd go through with a hand fork and put them on to a cart and put these into another field: where we were going to have the mangels. The roots would be the first covering of the mangels.

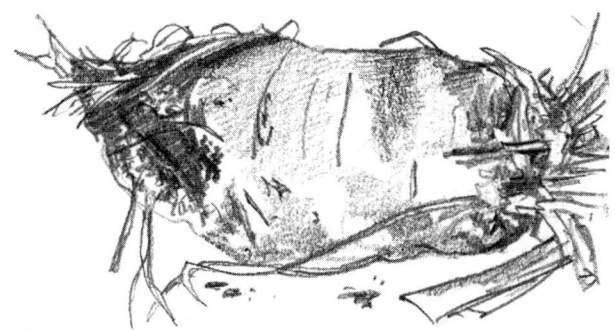

The mangel.

You'd cover them with about two feet of the roots. It had to be deep enough so you could put your fork in and couldn't feel them. Then the straw [the roots] was covered with a layer of hedge cuttings. These had been cut and left in the field where you had your 'cave', which would be as near to the farmhouse as you could get it.

We'd pull up the mangels or the turnips by hand in October or November; cut off the leaves and stalks, but not too close to the mangel because you'd 'bleed' them. The crop would go one side of the row and the greenery the other. The foliage wasn't wasted; it was spread over another field for the cows and sheep to eat, but mainly the cows. The cattle would eat sliced roots, corn and grain too.

The horses would collect these crops with their butts. You'd go one side and collect the crop, fill the butts and then back to collect the greenery.

The fodder could be put into a shed in the yard if there was room *or* a protected spot, which was called a 'mangel cave'. It would be where a frost wouldn't happen and usually against a hedge in a field. If they became frosted they would rot; they were mainly water.

When the shed stock became low you'd go out into the field and collect more. This would be eaten from the troughs by the cows. We would take this out to the field for the sheep; it had a certain amount of water, so it was good for all of them.

The turnips were purple in colour and you could eat it raw. Many a time, I've skinned one and eaten it. You could take the Swede-turnip to the shops and sell them. I can remember cutting them all up. There was a merchant. He'd bring empty sacks for you to fill. You'd put the best in and the merchant would collect a ½ cwt bag, [25.4kg].

You'd do the same with the cabbage, but the cows would eat these as well, from their troughs in the cowsheds, but only in the winter time.

The cabbage, flat pole cabbage[103] was *big*; we'd grow *acres of them*. They weren't grown from seed; they were bought as plants from another farmer. That was 'is job; 'e'd grow acres and acres of them. You'd drop them in row by row. We'd plant them by hand and dig them all in.

You'd cut them out of the ground with a chopper or hook more likely. You'd leave some of the stump in the ground so there was no earth on the cut part: the plant was clean to eat. You'd get rid of more of the stump, chop it through both ways and that would start to separate it and the cows would do the rest!

A merchant, Ted Snell, over at Bishops Tawton,[104] came for them. He'd collect the nice-sized ones and they'd be sent up to London and other places during the war. The cabbages were good to eat. I used to take them home quite a lot.

We used to grow *acres* of kale as well. While the cows were being milked, the kale, cabbage or Swede-turnip would be put in the field for them. A horse and cart would take it out and one of us would spread it along... a long row.

'You wouldn't plough up a hill with one horse'

Ploughing would be done before Christmas, probably in November. The fields were left to 'lay' and the frosts would help break up the soil even more. They would be left until February or March time. The winter frosts would kill any weeds that came up, but if we didn't need the field, we wouldn't harrow it.

There were different types of plough: the digger would dig up to six inches and the weeds would be buried deep and would rot. The long-plate was the skimmer plough and there was the Syracuse.

You'd dig before the frosts. The Huxtable 'One-Way' was a digger plough. The long-plate plough would skim the ground rather than dig into it. The long-plate and digger ploughs were pulled by two horses and were used in big fields: about twenty acres or more.

The digger plough was easier to work, because it would dig deeper than the long-plate or skimmer plough. If the horse went too fast, the skimmer could come out of the ground and you'd miss a bit!

The Huxtable was the main plough for digging; we could use the One-Way[105] for the steep fields. We'd make two furrows: one down and one up. It ploughed 'one way', but there was a lever, so when you got to the end, you pressed it with your foot and the plough would actually turn over and plough up the other way.

The skimmer plough was as big as the One-Way, but it was used after the corn had been cut, 'cos you didn't need to plough so deep.

You'd use a Syracuse,[106] on a *very steep* field with *one* horse. The gardeners would use a Syracuse plough. This *was* a digger plough and it was used for the main digging, but it was used for ploughing small fields... about an acre. You could use it in a garden if it was less than an acre. It would take longer to use 'cos it only had a small plate; it was set and you couldn't turn it.

We used to say, "You'd plough down light and up leary.[107]" That meant that the Syracuse would be laying on the ground. You wouldn't plough up a hill with one horse; it'd be hard work! So you'd walk back up to the top of the field without ploughing and then you'd put it in to action again coming down. It was easier for the horse this way.

When you were ploughing on steep ground, you'd couple the horses further apart, so when they turned, they'd keep going and wouldn't get caught on the loosened chains. You'd keep a wrench handy. There was a proper place on the handles of the plough for the wrench, for any nuts that went loose.

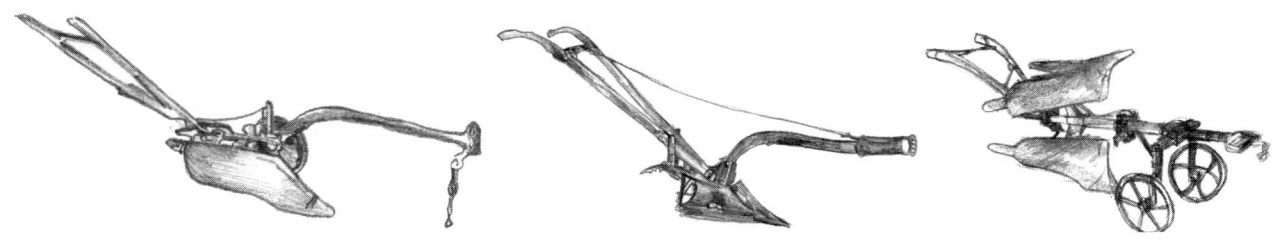

Ploughs: 'the Skimmer', 'the Syracuse', the 'Huxtable 'One-Way',

---

103 A West Country newspaper, 1836, reported that one weighed up to '39lbs and some ounces': 85.8kilos.
104 The village of Bishops Tawton lies south of Barnstaple, 15 miles from Berrynarbor.
105 Developed by John Huxtable & Son Ltd, Alexandra Plough Works, Barnstaple, in 1873, and followed by his 'Turnover plough' in 1889.
106 The Syracuse Ploughing Company began to export these ploughs from the USA in about 1890. Later, the company was acquired by a growing American business: John Deere.
107 'Leary', meaning 'empty, unladen'.

◈ FARMING LIFE ◈

Walking with a scuffle.

You had to keep the nuts oiled but they'd come loose when you were moving and rattling along. You had to know what you were doing; ploughing on steep ground, was *much* more difficult than on flat ground.

Harrowing broke up the soil, but we used a scuffle[108] before it was harrowed; the scuffle went deeper than the harrow. We rolled the furrows, loosened the soil with metal drags[109] behind two horses, but you worked a lever and it could dig to any depth you wanted: about a foot' [30cm]. Then you rolled it again. We used to keep spare 'feet' for the harrow, if they broke off: tangs[110] we'd call 'em on the farm.

You'd harrow, chain harrow, it to bring up any stones that were there. This was many rings linked into one another in a long line and they'd rattle along behind the horse. Once you'd harrowed the manure into the ground, you'd go along, two of you, to collect the stones: the bigger ones. These would be picked up and put in buckets. You had to collect these because they could damage the knives on the machinery. You'd leave the small ones to warm the ground in the ploughed field, but you'd pick up *every one you could see* in a grass field.

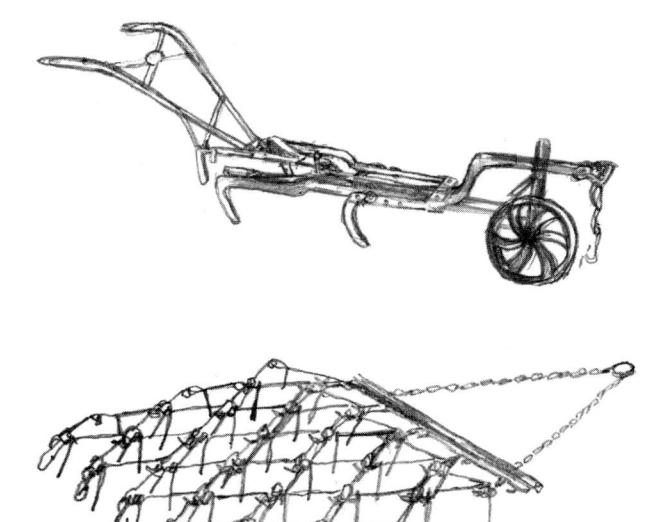

Top: *Scuffle.*
Above: *Chain or drag harrow.*

---

108 'A type of horse-drawn hoe with large tines used to break up heavy ground.'
109 'A drag harrow: a type of harrow consisting of heavy beams, often with spikes inserted, used to crush clods, level soil, or prepare seedbeds.'
110 'the pointed end of a tool, such as a chisel, file, knife, etc., which is fitted into a handle, shaft, or stock.'

Horses and chain harrow at Hangman Hills and Lester Point, Combe Martin.[111] Raphael Tuck & Sons
'This was on Newberry Farm. It was Jack Williams' land. He wasn't a well man, so I used to help him sometimes.'

'...better for the soil...'

We used to have manure and slag;[112] they were different things altogether. The slag was bought from the same merchant that sold the manure [fertiliser]. The slag was a black sooty colour, heavier than soot and like powder. It was put on arable ground: used mainly on poor grass fields. The Boss would say, "We need something to liven it up. We must get the slag on that field. It looks as if it's going to rain." He'd be right!

You'd sow it *before* it rained and the rain would help to work this in. We'd have one horse pulling a long box [at right angles] to the back of the horse and we'd walk behind. The same drill would sow the slag and the lime.

If we began it when it was mild at the beginning of the day we had to continue if it was wet and windy and we'd be black from head to foot! You couldn't do anything about it if it went in your face; you had to get on with it! We would sow it inside the wheel so to speak: forwards and backwards or else you'd miss a strip and you could see where you'd sown.

It was spread onto short grass too. Once it had started to grow you'd chain harrow it, then it was left so that hay could be made. When it *was* growing *nothing* was allowed in there. The grass would be much better for making the hay or feeding the sheep.

On cold wet days you could repair the wooden hay loft: the planks of wood for the floor. You could put your foot through a board if it was rotten... dry rot and worm eaten.

We wouldn't have people coming round to check. You've got to have this guarded and that guarded today. There was nothing like that in my young day!

The hay loft was above the stables and the cow sheds. The bullocks and the horses were here in winter. If the hay went off, there'd be a lot of dust when you started to move it. The cough, the husk[113] *we'd* call it, would make the cows and the workers cough.

---

111 The 'Point' is known as Lester Point.
112 A local farmer said: 'You can still get it. It comes from iron foundries. It's come into its own again...it's good for the ground. Slag and lime do the same job, but lime makes an acid soil alkaline. Slag has more trace elements. Both make the grass sweeter and improve the soil.
113 'bronchitis in cattle, sheep and goats, usually caused by lungworm infestation'.

In the snow, the sheep would go into the weather; they'd go for the *wrong* hedge: where the snow was beating right in. They'd get *covered!* They *never* went for the shelter, but we say, "As maze[114] as a sheep."

The dogs would know where to find them. The sheepdogs would *dig in*. They seemed to sense where they were and make a hole, and then you'd work with a spade to get the sheep out.

The cows would go under the trees. If it was going to be good, they'd be up on the hill for the breeze. People don't use the signs now...

We'd look after the horse machinery in the winter. It was put into the implement shed and in wet weather you could go in there, scrape off any rust, paint and oil it.

We didn't have Shires and we didn't have a big enough stable for all of them, so just two of them would be in the stables, over winter, between November and April, but we didn't always use the same two. The Horseman looked after the team.

We didn't have horses with long tails either; the Horseman would cut their tails, then they wouldn't affect the guides, the rope reins, when they swished their tails. The horse hair was more money for the Horseman. Gypsies came round and paid you for the hair.

'we would steep them over'

We'd never do hedging or ditching if the frosts were about. If you cut wood when there was a frost it would split, but we'd do the hedging and ditching in the winter months.

If it was a damp day, not pouring hard, you'd put a sack round your shoulders. You'd work your way down the hedge both sides; you'd pare down the sides and the top.

We used to create a bank from the edge of the field to the hedge with turf, which was cut from the edge. You'd slope the turf up to the hedge. It would fill holes in a hedge, like a grass bank, and it'd be about four feet high [approx.120cms].

The first piece was cut with an old-fashioned shovel, then there'd be the next piece and the next, but you had to slope it gradually otherwise it'd slip down. You couldn't do this on a frosty day: the turf would be too hard. You could go into a neighbour's field, if you had to, but you weren't allowed to cut too much away.

If there were any large trees in the hedge you'd cut 'em right out, but the wood would be used for firewood. We also cut crooks from these to keep the hedge down. We'd drive them in and it would keep everything down and tidy.

We cut the hedge and then we would *steep* them over: bend the branches over one way. What could be used for laying or steeping was left.

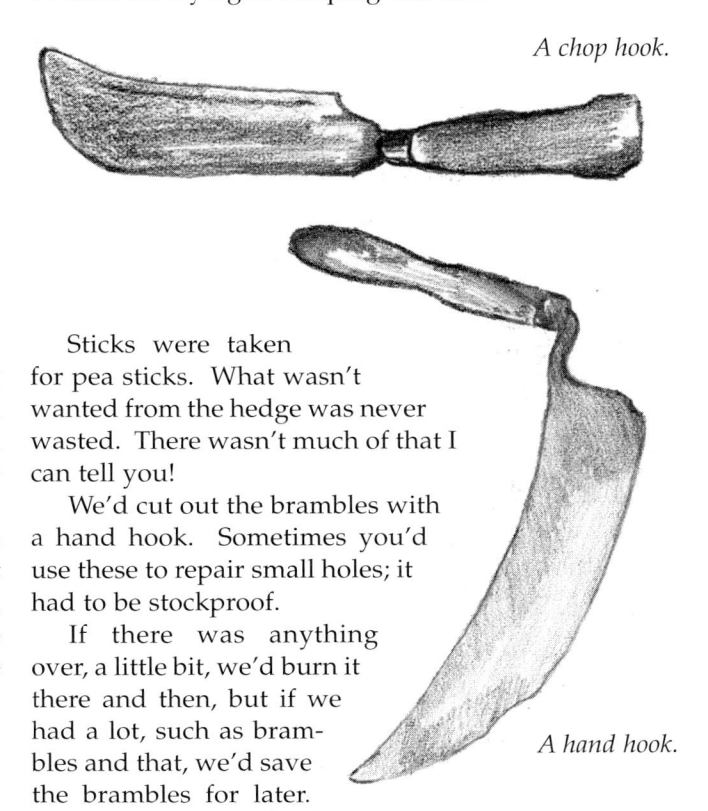

A chop hook.

Sticks were taken for pea sticks. What wasn't wanted from the hedge was never wasted. There wasn't much of that I can tell you!

We'd cut out the brambles with a hand hook. Sometimes you'd use these to repair small holes; it had to be stockproof.

If there was anything over, a little bit, we'd burn it there and then, but if we had a lot, such as brambles and that, we'd save the brambles for later. We'd make a big pile of these and keep them for months. They helped to stop rats getting to the corn and hay and they'd be used to keep the crops off the ground: to stop them from rotting.

A hand hook.

About 4.30 in the afternoon one of us would go and get the horse and cart to collect all the brambles. They'd be spread on the ground, under the ricks, in the yard and the fields, and the corn or the hay would be put on top.

If the bullocks had been charging about, they'd damage the hedges: tear them down. They had horns then; they were dangerous, you had to watch them. We'd use two rows of barbed wire along the hedge to stop the bullocks from tearing it down, but when it was very hot, they'd still go to the hedge to get the earth to throw over their heads to cool theirselves.

The wire was stapled to the posts and these were driven in to the hedge with a hammer. The wire would be far enough apart; they could get all of their head in, but not down to their necks.

Cows are crafty; they would try and knock the fence over. When they knocked it over they'd have a chance to get to the crops.

---

114 For Ron this means 'silly', but 'maze' is derived from 'amaze': 'an obsolete word for bewilder'...

Some would ignore an electric fence! If they tried it once they didn't do it again, but if their horns got caught, they could pull a whole lot of it out. The Devons were all born with the possibility of horns.

Albert Jones used to come to Home Barton to help out and he could hold on to the electric fence. We thought it was fun to try, but *he* could do it, but if you touched him you'd get a shock from him!

'it was handy for feeding the animals'

Another bad weather job was to grind all the feed for the pigs and the cattle. We used to breed and sell the small pigs to the villagers; everyone had a pig in them days. We had a few at Middle Lee... to eat. We had quite a few pigs on Home Barton; they were in sheds around the farm and they used to roam wherever they wanted. They'd go from Barton Farm and over the road[115] to where Napps is.

Pigs ate *anything*. We'd grind the oats down for the corn meal, which was rougher than barley meal and used for cows and the pigs and we'd add sliced-up mangels with their meal and mash.

We'd move the oats, the corn, from the hutches with a big tin spade shaped at the sides and it would be tipped down the chute to the hopper and ground by the mill below. The linney[116] mill could be moved around, but it had one job – grinding the corn.

When it was ground, it went into sacks. Another man'd watch the sacks fill, take away the full sack, then put another one on. A trap door used to stop the flow. This was usually done on a wet day, but if we were running out we'd *have* to do it, whatever the weather.

The sacks were taken to the storage shed that we had for feed. This was next door to the shippen, so it was handy for feeding the animals. We'd take it out to the shed in the sacks and then it was tipped from the sacks into big bins. You'd be able to reach down and get it.

You had to put it in the wooden buckets to feed the cows. Bowls would be in the buckets and you'd go round and feed them.

The pigs' trough was just inside the stone-built pig house, 'cos they had some weight behind their noses. It couldn't be tin or wood because they'd break this or try to root it up from underneath, but their rings would stop them!

The sows could be very nasty, particularly if they had young; they'd go for you, but the boars had tusks, so a rope would be put behind their teeth and you'd put a strong rope over a crossbeam and wait for their front legs to come off the ground. Then you'd use a saw to cut off the tusks and they'd be thrown away.

If the cows or horses didn't have good teeth, or the calves had soft teeth, we'd put vegetables into the slicer, the scrauncher, not mixed: one crop at a time. We knew what each cow liked and we'd look after them.

The scrauncher was made of iron and you'd turn a handle and the blades around the edge would slice them up. We'd do this with turnips, mangels and the potatoes too... separately. The potatoes were only cut if they were big. They weren't wanted by people but the cows would chew the sliced-up potatoes.

'to come and prepare the birds.'

Turkeys, chickens, ducks and geese were killed when they were wanted, but a couple of months before Christmas we'd bring so many into the rick yard for Christmas. We'd pick out a couple of pigs for Christmas too. They'd be kept in the yard all the time and given a bit of extra food and clean water every day, 'cos if they were running around they wouldn't get fat!

When we wanted to fatten up the geese, we'd pick out some and bring them in: mainly the ganders; we'd get new ones for the next year. You'd bring a certain number of chickens in too; you'd use the older ones for fattening up. They weren't marked up or anything, but you knew which ones to use just by looking at them.

We'd feed them up with mainly potato mash and barley meal mixed, in their troughs. It was a special meal, more like a powder and bought from merchants in Barnstaple. We could add corn too: the oats.

They'd fight in the rick yard because it was a smaller place than they were used to. We'd put them in separate poultry houses at nights. The turkeys and the chickens would fly up high.

For most of the year they'd be running around, during the day they'd usually stay in their own groups. When they were together normally they might fight for a bit when they were in at nights, but the turkeys would roost high where there were perches and the geese and ducks would sleep on the ground; they'd squat anywhere. We'd go out, just as

---

115 These pigs were traversing what is now a busy holiday route: the A399 runs from South Molton at Aller Cross, through Brayford, Combe Martin and to Ilfracombe.
116 *'Southwest English dialect,* a lean-to-shed.'

it was getting dimmet.[117] We'd find them around in the field near the yard, and on the carts. If we did forget one night we never had any trouble, but there were more rabbits for the foxes then!

There were no doors to the cart shed, so we had to drive them into their own houses. They'd roost on the carts, especially on the shafts, if they could, and on the butts and their mess would get all over your hands if you didn't see it when you went to take the carts or the butts out in the morning, so we had to chase them out with a dog before they settled!

In the morning, the geese would fly out to the grass fields. They'd fly to get going: morning exercise!

Their sheds were in the cart shed, the linney. It was always called the linney in my day… It was a big square building – a shed with space for all the carts and butts. You could put one cart over the shafts of another; it would give you the room. They had to be kept in else they'd rot in the rain. The shed was big enough for three carts; no door, just an opening and the sacks of manure and that would be put to one side.

The stag turkeys and the ganders could be vicious; they could be dangerous at any time. They would fly over you – particularly the turkeys; and the ganders would go for your legs! When they were mating they could be *really* nasty then.

All the farm hands would be expected to come and prepare the birds. This was the main job on the farm this time of year. Emma, the Missus, would do *any* woman's job, so she'd remove the insides. They had to be careful not to break the skin; if it was, they'd have to knock a penny or two off.

People would pay a bit extra to have them plucked. The turkeys weren't white; they were bronze.

'You could tell when the ewes were ready'

When the ewes came into season, we'd paint the ram with a particular colour of paint: a proper sort of paint for the job. We'd put it on his chest, so that when he was rising to serve the ewe, the paint would come off on to her. We'd leave him with that colour and we'd check it every other day. After about three weeks, we'd give him a different colour. We'd know from the colour when the ewe was due to lamb.

You couldn't put more than one ram in a field: they'd go for each other. You could tell when the ewes were ready: they'd be all around the ram. The ewes would be left for about four months before the lambs were born.[118] The ewes wouldn't allow the ram to serve them again: once was enough!

We would feel the sheep: feel their udder to see if it was beginning to rise or we'd feel their underneath to see if they were 'in lamb'. You'd turn them up: put their heads under yours, almost, and sit them down on their behind; *that* wasn't easy. You'd feel around their teats to make sure there was milk there.

'it was good for the ground'

Lorries would deliver small pieces of lime and powdered lime[119] from merchants in Barnstaple, before we needed it. Sack loads were used on the farms; it was ploughed in and put on ground and grass. You'd plough first, harrow it over and then sow the lime. If it rained, it was just the job 'cos it would wash it in! It was good for wireworm too: to protect the potatoes. It was put into the buildings and used outside for the limewash; the horses and farm butts carried it all.

Farmyard manure, dung, we used to call it, was straw and bits of all sorts. It would be loaded in the farm butt. One man with a horse and a fork would put it in piles, five paces apart: one pile would meet another when you went to spread it. You'd spread it with a fork on the grass fields then ploughed it in, then left for it a while before we sowed. This took several days. It had to be ploughed in while the manure was wet; it would be hard to turn over if it was dry and was better for the soil if it was wet.

Manure, was used, mainly, for the arable fields, but the grass fields had it too. It was a fine powder, a fertiliser. It went on fields after we'd ploughed but before we'd sowed.

There was a merchant, Berry's of Barnstaple.[120] We had 2 cwt [approx. 100kgs] sacks of this manure and, usually, we used two sacks per acre but it depended on the farmer and the quality of the field. There were different types of manure too; you'd use one sort for grass and a different one for growing potatoes and the vegetables.

We would load up the horse and cart with five 2cwt bags, about ½ ton [approx. 500kgs]. If he had to go up hill it would be less, but if it was downhill or on the flat you could take ½ ton. You'd take it out to the field, let the horse out and take him back to the farm to collect the manure drill.

---

117 Devon dialect: 'dimmet, the dusk of the evening'.
118 The usual gestation period for a sheep is 148 days, or '5 months minus a week'.
119 A local farmer told me: 'It puts the nutrients back in the ground… makes the grass sweet.'
120 Berry & Sons Ltd were 'corn, cake & manure merchants & agricultural implement dealers' and were in Tuly Street.

One horse and the drill sowed it. We'd walk *miles!* The manure, the fertiliser, would be put into a drill, a long narrow box, V-shaped. You'd turn a handle for the roller, which was at the bottom of the box to set it. The horse moving along would turn the cogs on the rollers and the manure would go down the box onto the field.

You wouldn't miss a bit; your mind had to be on your work. You had to use a quiet horse, 'cos the gates weren't wide enough to take the drill into the field; you'd have to get the drill in bit by bit.

If the horse was trained well, he'd hold the load and he'd sit well back, in the briching,[121] around his behind; his weight and position would hold the load and the cart. On a hill, you'd *hold* them back; they'd know what to do and they'd be holding *some* weight at times.

Briching would be used when the horses had a cart or a farm butt: something to hold. It went below their tails around the back of their behinds. They had a belt that would go under their stomachs, near his front legs. There was a strap for each horse. The square, padded saddle, not a riding saddle, was on the horse and the chains went through a hole in the saddle and they were fixed to the shafts of the cart.

When they stood back, that would stop the load moving; it would act like a brake, but you still had to keep your eye on them until we *all* got used to each other: the different machinery, the harnesses and that. When you'd finished, you'd back the cart in, to the linney, let the horse out, take the horse to the stable and take off his harness.

'There was always a man behind the thresher,'

Mostly, the corn was black oats. You don't hear of it now. The seed heads *were* black. You'd go out for two or three hours before threshing to check if the corn stooks were wet. If they were then you'd turn them from the inside to the outside; they'd be put to the sun, but the cord was left on. The damp sheaths of corn would be left for another day.

Threshing was done in the winter on a dry day. It was the *only* time we'd go into the farmhouse. Emma, the Missus, would have a proper cooked meal for us at 1 o'clock. If you went to any other farm you'd get a cooked meal too.

Emma wouldn't do it by herself; she had someone to come in and help a couple of days a week. Me mother used to go and help the Missus, in the house: scrubbing the floors, doing the polishing and dusting the ornaments, but when we were threshing she'd always have help. There'd be a lot of us there: could be up to eight to ten men!

We'd have one or two at the back to unhook the sack when it was full. When they were changing the sacks, we'd put a shutter down to stop the corn flowing; two would take the sacks away, fix another sack and then start it flowing again... There was always a man behind the thresher, in the field or the yard, and it was his job to keep his eye on the corn sack. When the sack was filled, he would shut down a lever to stop the corn coming out; it would be coming out fast.

The filled sacks would then be taken away on our backs and up the steps to the granary. The granary was above the linney. We used to carry the sacks of grass seed, pig meal, the corn, cow cake and the chicken food to the granary. It all had to be *off* the ground.

Two men would work in the granary; they'd be farm hands that worked on the farm all the time 'cos they had to walk up the twelve or fourteen steps with heavy sacks to the granary; there were no guards or handrails, but I never knew of any accidents! There'd be about three bushels[122] in a sack that were filled with the threshed corn.

The granary had three or four hutches; the threshed corn, the oats, was in the hutches. You'd take one, tip it in and go back for more. These'd be big enough to stand in to turn the corn. You could smell it if it was warm; you could feel the heat from it. You had to keep turning it.

If it went off, we'd call it 'vinnied'; it would be brown. You couldn't sow this; it would be ground down for the bullocks. They had this when they were laying in, in the winter months.

We'd grow black oats, white oats and small peas together too in a nine or ten acre field. We'd grow these with broad beans, which were the small, proper cattle beans; the peas were for cattle too. When they were all mixed together, it was called a dredge and was cut with a horse-drawn mowing machine. It looked pretty grown together in them days.

It was treated like ordinary corn; the whole lot would be put into the thresher. The peas and beans would take longer to be threshed, but the peas, beans and corn would go one way and the straw would go the other. The straw would be thrown out of the thresher into bundles and they'd be put into a rick. The straw ricks were in the rick yard and they could also go in the hay loft.

---

121 Ron's pronunciation of 'breeching': the strap of an all-leather harness, passing around the horse's haunches.
122 1 bushel is 'a British unit of dry or liquid measure equal to 8 Imperial gallons' or about 36.4l.

◈ FARMING LIFE ◈

You had to watch it because the peas and beans would fly into your eyes. There was no safety gear, nothing like today. We should have worn glasses, but we didn't!

The rubbish, the douse,[123] would drop down under the thresher. You could take it out into the field and the cows would take the best of it.

A chaff cutter would cut the straw. You didn't mind corn growing tall then, 'cos you knew you could use all of it. You fed horses more with the chaff[124] than you did the bullocks. You could add some corn to the chaff for the horses' feed. The straw was used for bedding too. The corn could be about three feet [90cms] high; I haven't seen any tall corn today, but the straw isn't the only thing they use for bedding today.

When the hay sheds were low, on a dry, calm day, you'd take a horse out with a cart, load it, bring it in from the open ricks, the ones in the field and fill them, 'cos you'd want hay right handy. When the two men were making the open ricks, they'd be spreading it about, but they'd be standing on it and treading it down, so it was harder to cut out than you'd think.

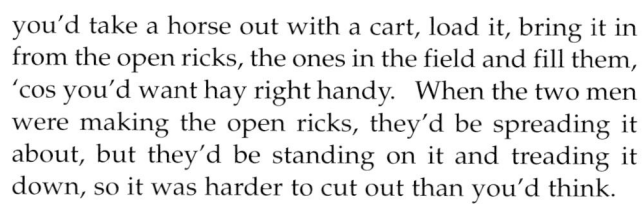

You had to take a hay knife to it to cut some out. It was under the reeds, but you wouldn't remove all of *them*. There'd be a wooden ladder by the rick, but you couldn't leave that there all year round 'cos it'd rot. The hay from the sheds would be taken to the hayloft so it was ready for the cow sheds and the stables.

In the winter, the bullocks were outside and the cows were milked inside. You had to feed up the bullocks before going home. We'd go home about 6.00 or 6.30pm for dinner.

'Spring Was Lambing Time...'

You'd leave the field over winter, but you'd keep working it to get rid of the weeds and plant in the springtime: when the weather had warmed up a bit. Before you could plant, you'd 'plum it up': you'd make the soil very fine.

You'd make the ground loose by ploughing it first: about six to eight inches deep; and you'd plough the whole field. Then you'd roller it a couple of times to flatten it.

Then you'd 'arrow it and roll it, break up all the lumps to get the soil *very* fine. When you were 'arrowing, you'd use a pair of iron drags; they helped till the soil. They were two frames about four feet wide, linked together with spikes about six inches long, you'd go over it again. You could change the frame around and once you'd planted you'd use it the other way and it would turn over the soil but it wouldn't dig up the plants.

When the soil was ready you sowed the seed, but this wouldn't be done until the Boss had put his toe into it. If he could bury his toe it was all right! Nowadays, they plough and sow it right in. I think it was better then... to leave the soil. We didn't use sprays then.

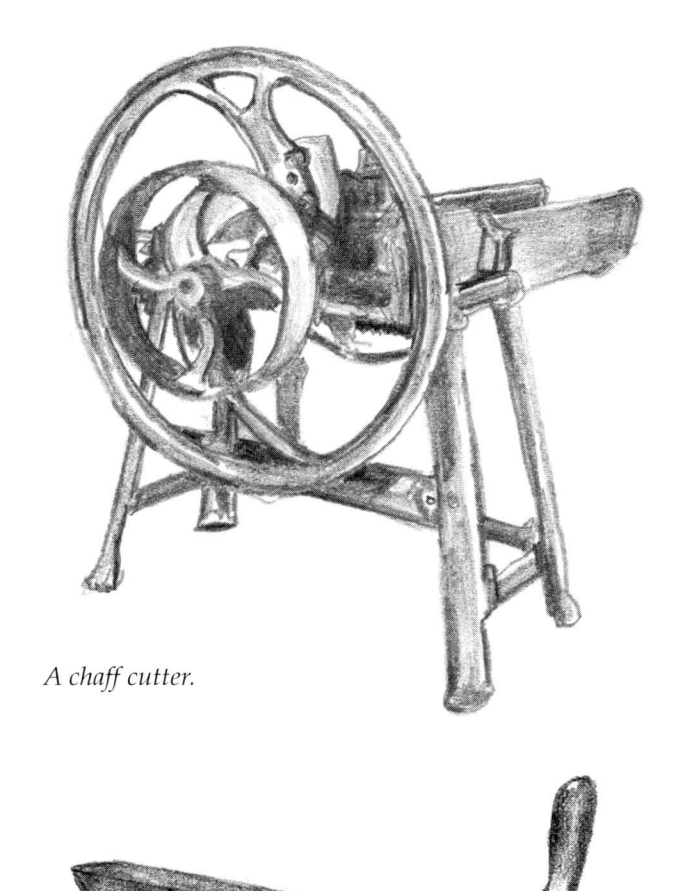

A chaff cutter.

A hay knife.

---

123 Devonshire dialect: 'douse' is 'dust – especially that from threshing'.
124 'chaff': 'the mass of husks, etc., separated from the seeds during threshing...finely cut straw and hay'.

'our corn was the loose corn'

Usually, we'd buy new corn every year, but we'd save some of our own. The corn merchants were in Barnstaple: Trumps[125] were corn and seed merchants. Their delivery lorries had *hard* tyres and the sacks could be a hundredweight [1cwt or 50.8k] or 2cwt.'

Trumps Ltd.

A seed drill.

'They'd have two on a lorry and they weren't young men. I knew one who was getting on in years. He could sit up and drive the lorry, but *he was bent*. I suppose he was bent from delivering... They had a lot to get round. They'd deliver at the end of the week: usually on a Friday. They came to us on a Friday anyway. They would leave the sacks in the linney and drop them on the floor. They weren't too pleased if no-one was there to help them: the sacks were heavy!

If you were going to use it soon you'd leave the sacks in the linney, but it couldn't be in the sacks too long in the linney; it would get damp. The linney had an earth floor; we used any bits of wood around so everything was stored about four inches [10cms] off the ground.

The corn, and the manure, had to be dry so it would flow through your fingers, and the drill, as you were sowing it. It was really good corn and could be left in the sacks for about a week. Some of it could be the corn you were going to sow for next year's crop, so you *had* to take them up the steps to the granary; two of you would do it. We'd keep the best of ours too, underground, to sow the next year; this would save you *pounds and pounds*.

The seed was sown by machine, which was a box on wheels. Horses pulled it but it was hoed [weeded] by hand. You had to know how much seed to use. You could use your own seed when you were sowing corn, but our corn was the loose corn and was kept in the hutches.

When you needed it, you took the sacks down from the granary and put it into a horse cart and took it out to the field.

You'd leave the sacks by the hedge. When you wanted the corn, you'd use one, take another then another. You'd put them so far apart and when the drill was empty, you'd go to the hedge and fill it up again. It was going down the tubes that went just above the ground. The plum ground would fall back into the holes to cover the seed.

'If the weeds won't grow, nothing will!'

Seed wouldn't be sown so deep. If you were sowing small seeds, mangels or turnips, you put these seeds into a drill, which had two wheels and a long box: the chute. The [horizontal] chute had half-a-dozen pipes, about 9 inches apart [23cms] which went down into the soil. The seeds would be in the chute. When the wheels turned, they turned the cogs and the seeds went down the pipes into the soil. The pipes would be *full* of seeds!

You had to try and set it so that not too many seeds fell out at once, but it was never one seed in those days; it could be half a dozen, so there was a lot wasted. You had to go back later, when they'd grown a bit, and use the long, wooden-handled hand hoes to kill the weeds and take out the plants you didn't want: one plant in one hole! You could spend several days taking out the unwanted plants.

You'd hoe on a dry day; you had to go back and use the hand hoes to kill the weeds. You couldn't leave the weeds, they'd choke the plants!

---

125 'Wholesale & import seedsmen & corn manure merchants,' and had their head office in the High Street. They were also 'wool merchants'.

FARMING LIFE

In the cornfields, when the corn appeared, six men would walk up and down and take out the weeds, but these were mainly the thistles. We called them dashels.[126] There were horse dashels and sheep dashels. The sheep dashels were the smaller thistles, not the big flowering type. You had to get these out otherwise they'd seed and spread.

The horse dashels could be three feet high [90cms] high, but they had pretty purple flowers. They were prickly mind, but I'd take a bunch home to my wife when I was married.

What weeds came up we hoed by hand. We'd use long-handled weeding irons, like a hoe, but it [the metal head] had to be smaller so we didn't dig up the corn. We used to say, 'If the weeds won't grow nothing will!

'and then the potatoes would be left'

Potatoes used to be planted in February and March. The Boss would decide how many acres to plant up. Usually, we had about fifteen acres for potatoes, but if he wanted ten acres in a bigger field, he'd measure it out with a long stick; it was half a rod.[127]

He'd hold the stick upright with one end touching the ground; he'd walk with it, pointing it forward and lowering it towards the ground. When the top end touched the ground, he'd use this spot and lift the stick from here, upwards, then lower it forwards again and again.

You'd plant by hand. We had wooden potato buckets to carry them in them days. Half-a-dozen men would plant up. Three would plant up half the row from one end and three would plant up the other half. You'd plant one row, miss a row, plant one row and miss a row all the way across the field.

At the beginning of one type of potato you planted a few garden beans: broad beans. At the beginning of the next type of potato you'd plant more beans. The beans separated the types of potato and were another crop. You'd pick the beans when they were ready, but you'd leave the stalks so you'd know where the potatoes were. The Boss used a book to write down the names of the types of potatoes.

You had to plant every other row because you had to leave space for the horse to come through with the plough or the 'arrow. When you'd finished planting one row, one horse, man and plough would come through and bury that row.

It used to take a day: between 9am to 1pm and 2pm to 5pm to do an acre and a half and we'd have to take the horses back to the farm for something to eat and drink at lunchtime too. Today they can use a tractor and plant four rows at a time.

As soon as you saw the weeds you'd get on to them. You'd dig them up and leave them lying there to die. Nature would do its work: the sun would kill them; you wouldn't collect them! You'd get on to the weeds whatever the crop.

One man with a horse and scuffle would go first, to get rid of the weeds. You'd scuffle then you hoed when the first plants appeared.

The scuffle was different from a horse hoe. The scuffle had long feet, so it went a bit deeper than the horse hoe *and* it *would* get rid of the weeds, but it would loosen up the soil too. The horse hoe was the main thing for removing the weeds.

Once the potatoes were about a foot high [30cms], you'd go through, one man with one horse with the scuffle. He'd go through between the rows. Then another man would come along and follow to bank them up. We'd be walking.

You'd bank them up with a drilling or

A horse hoe.

a banking plough. You only used a banking plough once and then the potatoes would be left. You'd clear the earth in the middle and it would be pushed up around the potatoes. You'd leave them for two or three months, once you'd banked them up.

You'd also have two or three men with hand hoes, going round *every* potato plant. The men from the village would help. Some men would take on one or two acres of hoeing by hand.

In the same field, he'd have potatoes, you planted the earlies, then the lates and next to those perhaps mangels or flat-pole cabbage. Then you'd leave all

---
126 Another dialectal example: dashels are milky-dashels or sow thistles.
127 Rods were the usual unit for assessing the length or area of land. Also known as a 'pole' or 'perch', it has a length of 5 ½ yards or approximately 5 metres.

the crops, but you'd keep scuffling, so the weeds would come out. There's part of a scuffle at the back of The Globe. It didn't matter if you couldn't see the weeds, the roots'd be there!

'he'd get the legs out.'

Spring was lambing time and the sheep'd be out in the fields. Lambing was only once a year then. When we knew the ewes were to lamb we'd move them into the rick yard, so we could keep an eye on them. You'd bring them as near to the farm as you could; you wouldn't always put them in a shed, particularly if it was a mild night. You'd *know* which *one* was to lamb *first.*

If it was a bad night, you'd get them close to the hedge. There was a hedge around the yard and there was a wide gateway, but we'd close it at nights to keep the sheep from going out.

We'd use lambing oil on our hands. If you saw just the lamb's head hanging out, you had to push the head back into the womb, feel about and grab the front legs and pull. You wouldn't *dare* pull the head; you could break its *neck*!

There weren't the vets in them days; the farmers would help each other. If you had a really difficult case, there was a man in the village: Ivor Richards was his name. He had a *very* small hand and arm and he'd get the legs out. You couldn't phone then, so you'd have to fetch him and he'd come and help. He wasn't the only one to do it but he was noted for his small hand.

It's all done in big sheds now, but we didn't then. Nowadays some farmers have cameras so they can see what's going on in their sheds!

'sowing and growing'

Late spring and early summer, May and June, was the time for the sowing and growing of crops, such as the cattle fodder: the mangels, the flat-pole cabbage and the Swede-turnip,[128] and the sheep shearing.

As soon as the Wild Garlic[129] came up, Ramseys we'd call it, we'd beat it down 'cos you tasted it in the milk if the cows got to it. When you saw it coming up you *had* to beat it down. You had to remove that yellow flower[130] too; this is death to the cows and horses.

You had to be careful about feeding the milking cows too many turnips as well. It would flavour the milk. You'd taste it! We'd get complaints now and again, so we had to be careful.

'during the summer...'

Before the sheep had to be sheared, if they had itchy backs, they'd roll over and then they couldn't get up, so a dog would pull at their wool or their leg. He'd get up, but he'd be a bit dizzy and wobble around.

You had to have eyes in the back of your head on the farm! If a crow, hawk or a rook saw a sheep on their back, they'd go for the skin on their backside. They wouldn't go for the wool!

Only one type of sheep was kept when I was on the farm and they were the Devon Closewools.[131] It had a tight, woolly fleece and most farmers round here had this type.

When the weather was right we would shear them by hand. It was never done when it was wet. They were sheared in a big barn, but if it was a *nice* day we would go out into a field and a pen would be put round and then we'd shear them in here.

The young Richards boys and a couple of men would come in from the village; they'd catch the sheep and pass them on to the shearer. Each farm did their own shearing, but some farmers helped each other.

There were no proper sheep–shearers; we'd just learn how to do everything. When I was living in we had to learn a lot of things. I can see my Boss now; he'd stand over me and say, "Do this… and …do that," and you'd try to do it, like shearing the sheep.

You would have to hold the sheep tight so that the skin was taut and then it was harder to cut! If you cut it, you'd know it!

A sheep would be sat down on its behind with its head up and you'd cut under its legs and around the stomach area. You would clean this area first and then the back, which was easier, so any loose bits would be wrapped up into the main fleece. Their

---

128 Swedish turnip, Brassica napus
129 Ramsons, Allium ursinum: a broad-leaved garlic and a European native. In May, this white-flowered plant can be found on banks, in hedgerows and along footpaths. Its leaves are an alternative to the purchasable garlic bulbs.
130 Common Ragwort: Senecio jacobaea L. This toxic weed causes liver damage and death to cattle and horses. This was one of 'five injurious weeds' listed in The Weeds Act 1959. Its dangers warranted the amendment of this Act to The Ragwort Control Act 2003. All landowners are expected to control it.
131 The Closewools were first seen on Exmoor. As their name suggests, their dense white fleece enables them to withstand its wind and rain, making them a natural choice for this moor; however, even these have been 'updated'. A local farmer has said that they are, "an old-fashioned variety. We keep Texels and North Country Mules now."

FARMING LIFE

Devon Closewool.

Texel.

North Country Mule.

Tying sheep fleeces.

fleeces would be taken off in one piece.

The lambs would be left until their wool was thick and then it was put into a sack. The inside would be facing the barn floor and it would be folded into itself; we would kneel on it; keep it tight; and tie it up with wool cord that you could buy in big bales. These would be put into big sacks, *really* big sacks, and then the sacks would be tied.

There weren't so many black sheep then and you had to keep their fleeces separate. I've heard that the black fleeces aren't so good as the white ones.

If sheep died on the farm you wouldn't ring somebody up to collect it; you'd bury it yourself. They'd be buried without their wool, so you'd leave it in the field for a few days but you'd cover it with a sack so the crows or seagulls couldn't get to it. Once the skin was 'ripe' the wool was easier to take off. The Boss would look after this until it was shearing time and it would be put together.

There were quite a lot of foxes around then, so you had to bury them deeply. Before the last layer of earth was put on, you'd put a layer of brambles to stop the fox from getting to the animal. There are tricks to every trade!

Wool merchants would come to collect them. Six sacks would be one load on the lorry and from one farm only. It would be taken to Barnstaple first and then it would go on.[132]

Some sheep would keep going through hedges and pull off their wool, so when you came to shear

---

132 Devon and Cornwall Wools, South Molton, is an amalgamation of smaller merchants, including one in Barnstaple. They are the main depot for this area and collect wool from as far away as Hampshire. 'Some farmers deliver their own wool... or we hire a haulier to collect. It hasn't changed much; some farmers still come with their tractor and trailer, unload, banter with the graders and bring their lunch.' All wool is sold through the British Wool Marketing Board's H.Q. at Wool House, Bradford. 'Small samples are sent... it's sold to carpet manufacturers here and we export: China and New Zealand. White fleeces can be dyed easily, black ones cannot.'

them there wasn't much left. I suppose it was a case of 'The grass is always greener!' They'd be easy to recognise though, 'cos of their initials.

Their initials'd disappear gradually, but after they were shorn somebody would mark them again. The marking irons were made by the blacksmith. The irons had the farmer's initials and they'd be dipped into tar. They all had initials. Ours had 'FR' – Fred Richards; other initials were 'WB' for William Bowden and 'WH' for William Huxtable.

On Exmoor there'll be hundreds of sheep grazing together, but the farmers'll know whose are theirs. They don't mark them with initials anymore; they just spray paint on them.

'they were...down for their holidays.'

During the summer we had to be careful with the visitors' children. The farm used to do B 'n B and the older children were often left. Their parents used to go off for the day; they knew they were safe, but they'd come back for dinner.

The children would follow me around in the mornings when I was going round feeding. Their parents could still be in bed, but the children would be down and could be a bit hindering. It was nice to see them, but they could get in the way!

Sometimes they'd amuse theirselves around the yard and the farm, but when we were shearing they'd be delighted to jump in the long sacks of sheep wool. There'd be forty to fifty fleeces and they'd jump in the long sacks and pack it down tight!

We had a big stone trough for the sows, so they couldn't move it... but they did! The children wouldn't go near the sows; they could be nasty, so they'd stand behind me. They could be *really* nasty when they'd just farrowed, even when you were bringing their food: their corn meal and cooked potatoes.

They'd watch me with the calves; you had to go into their sheds and the children would be right behind you. They were interested... they were the town children... down for their holidays.

They had to be told not to touch the geese. The geese and the ducks were out in the fields during the day but they used to come in to the yard to drink from the trough. The overflow water from the trough ran into a deep gutter and banked up so they could wash in it.

At night, the ducks and geese lived inside; they were shut away from the foxes in a tin shed, but it was still possible for a fox to get one. Their sheds were in the rick yard. All their eggs were sold...

We had to show them how to work the horses on the farm. They had to learn how to couple the horses together and chain them up: from the bit to the bit. They realised it was more difficult than they'd thought. You'd got to be quick to couple them together and to put the chains on, especially, the colts: the young ones.

When we were harvesting, they liked to ride out on the carts when they were empty; they liked this the best. They never helped with the hay making; you had to know what you were doing with a full load and going through a gate. When the cart was empty, they'd ride back from the hayricks to the rick yard. You'd have three or four horses and the carts; they'd be to-ing and fro-ing all the time.

'scooping up the hay and pitching it'

At harvesting time, the hay or corn harvest, the Boss would go into the village and knock on people's doors to ask for extra help, when it was all done by hand. The men in the village would be at work, but the Boss knew they'd be willing to come up in the evenings. When their husbands came in, their wives would tell them that they were wanted. They'd have a meal at home and come up.

The language used to get a bit heated, but there was no moaning or groaning: nothing like that. It was nice to see other men. We'd get together, work hard and have a yarn.

They'd light up their pipes or cigarettes and keep working. The money wasn't much; it was 'bacca money!'[133] It was always known as 'bacca money'. They could be working until ten at night, but they'd still have a bit of supper with the Boss and the Missus and then go 'ome.

The hay was made as soon as it was dry... in the summer. When it was time for hay making, the mower with two horses would cut the hay. It would be cut in rows.

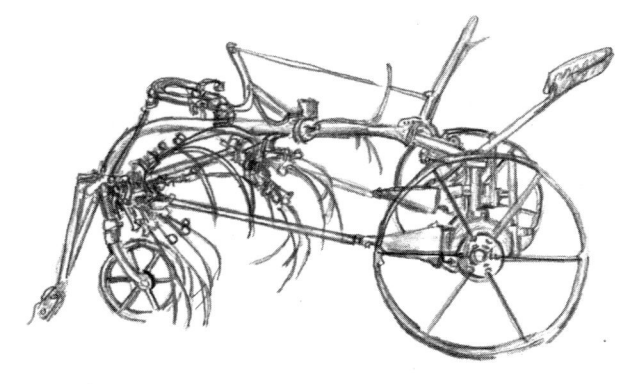

A swath turner.

---

133 'Tobacco money': additional cash.

◇ FARMING LIFE ◇

Pokes or stokes of corn. This was taken in 2010; it is a rare sight because these days it is usually baled.

Hangman Hills and Lester Point, Combe Martin c.1900. G.F. Beaumont
This view provides an illustration of how the corn fields once looked.

It would be left for a couple of days to dry and then it would be turned over with a swath turner and one horse,[134] which took two rows at a time. You'd go between the rows and the swath turner would turn it over completely for the bottom side to dry; it would turn two swaths or rows from thick end to thin. The thick end was the bottom of the grass; as it grew it was thinner at the top.

If the weather wasn't dry enough to put the hay or corn onto the cart, you'd put it into pokes or stokes, [stooks]. It was stacked in sixes and kept hollow so the wind could dry it. When it was good you'd spread it all over the field again.

You'd leave it for a couple more days to dry out and then we'd use the horse-drawn hay titter.[135] This was like the rake, but it really helped to dry it quickly. It had metal spikes; they *were* dangerous. It had a frame around it, a tin guard. It was always done on a *very* hot day. The spikes would lift it off the ground and it would be thrown high into the air; when it fell, it wouldn't lie flat on the ground.

You'd lift the hay to check it wasn't green anywhere; if it was you'd leave it again. When it was all over the field, you'd leave it for a few days and let it dry out, then you'd titter it again and collect it with one horse and a hay rake. You had to rake it up in rows; you'd pull a bit together, stack it up, just big enough for two men to lift it onto the cart, then on to a rick.

I was using a hay rake. This [opposite, top] was a photo of me. Jean Harper, who lived at Cross Park, painted made a painting of it [opposite, below]. This was off Barton Lane; it was mainly grass on the left side [as you go up and before the houses were built]. On the right is Hangman Hill.[136] This is up towards Home Barton, but the farmhouse is hidden.

Before we had the hay sweeps, we used hay rakes and the rest was done by hand. The hay would be propped up in rows and the horse would be put by the rows. The man on the cart, with the horse, would keep hold of the reins. You wouldn't put a young horse in for this job. If they did move, you'd say "Woh!" and they'd stop.

We'd have two or three carts and horses running backwards and forwards all the time, moving the hay from the fields to the rick.

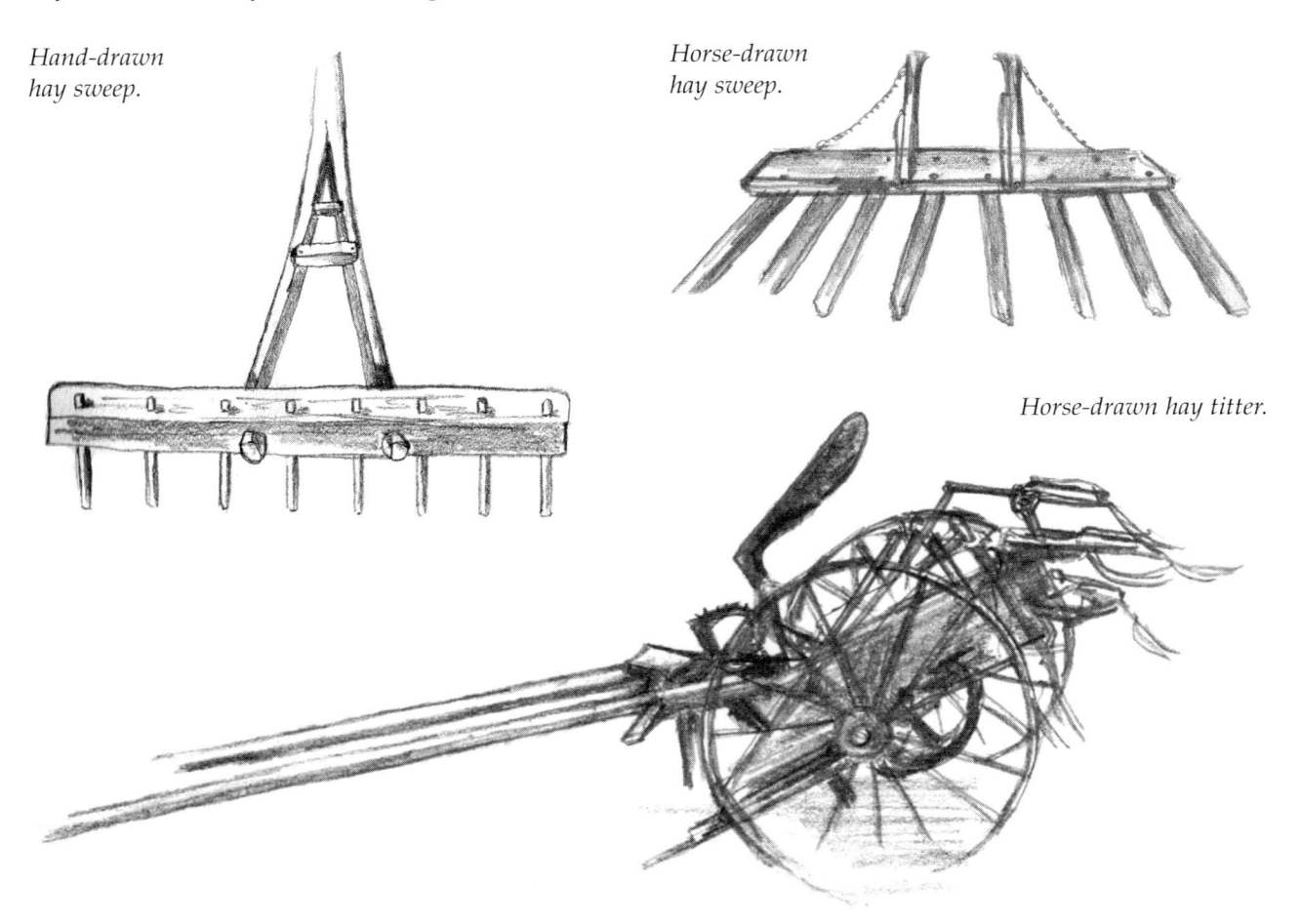

Hand-drawn hay sweep.

Horse-drawn hay sweep.

Horse-drawn hay titter.

---

134 Ron's pronunciation of a 'swath turner'. A 'swath' is the width, quantity or row of cut grass or hay made by one sweep of a scythe or of the blade of a mowing machine.
135 Ron's pronunciation of a 'hay tedder'. 'To ted' is 'to shake out and loosen, so as to dry it.'
136 At 318m or 1044ft, Great Hangman is the highest point on the South West Coast Path and is the highest sea cliff in mainland Britain.

◆ FARMING LIFE ◆

Ron with Noeleen seated on a hay rake.

Ron in field with horses.

'When you *were* harvesting, you had to use a wooden lade.[137] They were fitted front and back and they'd drop down into proper sockets so they fitted into the cart. It kept the hay off the horse and it wouldn't fall out at the back *and* you could take a lot more from the fields to the ricks.

There'd be two men in the field and it was their job pitching hay from the fields up to the carts. They'd use 'picks', long-handled two-prong forks, to lift the hay from the field onto the horse cart and a man on the cart would be treading the load in place and load up the cart evenly so it was balanced. He had to know his job to make a big load.

The horse cart would come alongside the rick. When you got to the rick, men would be there with their forks scooping up the hay and pitching it to the men on the ricks. There'd be another two making the rick.

The horse-drawn cart was used to move hay but on the steep roads or fields, you had to load it properly. I've seen many a load tip over; a load could take the whole lot over... the horse as well. It was only between two shafts and all harnessed up.

Years later, we had hay sweeps. The hay sweep was on the ground, attached to the horse with chains: to his neck collar. It had wooden spikes, about 1 foot [30cms] apart. It wasn't on wheels or anything. It was like a big wooden rack, with wooden crooks for the chains.

It would be collecting the hay, as you were walking behind the sweep, with guides: steering handles to drive the horse. It would be *piling up*, high enough for you not to see over the top. If you thought you had enough, you'd take it to the rick, raise the handles, the teeth would stick in the ground and you'd tilt the load to the side of the rick.

When the elevators came in, same time as the sweeps, they were worked by an engine. You'd put the hay at the bottom of it, with a pick, and the elevator would keep going up and down, to the top of the rick.

We had to have the extra help even when the elevators came in, but not so many. Two would be putting hay on to the elevator and two were on the top; one would be taking it off and passing it to the man making the rick.

'you could thatch the ricks in'

You'd make a big open rick, out in the field. You'd make a rick from one field. They'd be thatched in but they wouldn't get hot. They were *mainly* by the edge of a field, by a hedge that would shelter them from any storm. We'd cut brambles every year and the hay would be laid on top of the brambles and sticks on the ground, about two feet high, otherwise the hay or corn would rot. The weight of the crop made it drop down after a while, but it worked. The big square ones were left for the thresher to come around. They would sit and dry for some months. When the corn was dry it was threshed.

We had round ricks as well as the square ones. The round ricks were smaller so you could move the whole rick on to a cart and take them into the barn and use a barn thresher: a small machine. You wouldn't thatch these in but you'd put on a layer of straw and some poles on top. I don't think they make so much hay today. It's more silage[138] today.

You had to make the big hay ricks a bit like a 'V' shape, but it had a broad base and then you'd thatch it with reeds to keep the rain off. You had to know what you were doing; you wouldn't build them straight up; you'd start to run them off. The hay would be going outwards, not too much or they'd topple over, but the rain wouldn't run through the rick; it'd *run off*.

They'd be *proper* reeds, grown for the job that you'd buy from the merchants. When you bought the reeds, several bundles were delivered. Before we put them on we'd take them to a pond or stream and soak them; we'd stay with them for about ten to fifteen minutes. They were heavy when you were taking them out *and* the water was running out of them! They wouldn't slip if they were wet and you could thatch the ricks in.

To keep the hay in shape you'd use a tacker or patter. You'd pat the ends where they'd slipped down and pat them back into the shape. It was like a bat, cut from a piece of wood with a handle; it pushed it up and made a neat edge.

You'd tie it all in with proper thatching cord, across the thatch as you were thatching and you'd keep the ropes, the cord, in place with spars. We'd cut straight sticks, 'nut alz', we'd call 'em, cut from a hazel nut tree in the woodland. They'd be about two feet long, [60cms]; then we split them through, cut them downwards and bend them in half to make a V-shaped spar. They'd have sharp pointed ends. You'd put them in different places all over the thatch – not in rows. They'd go across the top of the cord.

We'd go inside to make the spars, in the winter or a wet day. There was always a job to do, *always*.

---

137 'lade', from the 'Old English *hladen* to load.'
138 'any crop harvested while green for fodder and kept succulent by partial fermentation in a silo.'

FARMING LIFE

Cutting grass before hay harvesting. Ron, standing with the scythe, and Stanley Harding, in their everyday working clothes. 'The sheepdog was Ben and the horses were Duchess and Tidy: on the right and left. We were scythe cutting the field, before hay harvesting, west of Barton Lane: the field below the houses, 'Red Tiles', 'Byways' etc. The little boy is John Willis, Bob Richards' cousin, who came to have his photo taken!'

'if it was really hot it would fizzle.'

There were two sheds that had the tin roofs and were opposite one another in the rick yard. The rick yard was just a dirt floor and uneven, but you'd find a level bit for the ricks. There was space between the sheds wide enough for the threshing machine to go through.

The Boss'd get an odd-job man in to help him to put posts in the ground and the frame for the galvanised tin roof over the top for the ricks in the yard, weeks before. To keep them waterproof, you'd paint the tin roofs with tar every year, but they'd *draw* the heat. You *had* to watch the ones in the yard.

We'd keep hay or corn in these sheds. They'd be used every year and would last *years and years*. When we were loading these ricks with the roofs, we'd pack it in at one end and work backwards; it had a tin back to it too, so you had to push it in.

These ricks would get *too* hot if there was too much green. My Boss would like to see a *bit* of green, but not too much; it would help to make the hay. He'd check using a metal rod; he'd push it into the ricks as far as it would go and leave it in for a few days. Then he'd pull it out every now and again to see if it was all right. He'd put his spittle on it and if it was really hot it would fizzle. He'd keep his eye on it. It would smell lovely in the winter if it was *good*.

There was space between the galvanised roofs and the hay. Sometimes it would get too hot; you could see the steam rising! We'd have to use a wooden ladder and put it at an angle to get into the top, into the middle of the hayrick and climb on to cut out a square hole with a hay knife to reduce the heat.

We'd remove the roofs and sometimes we'd have to remove the corn sheaves if they were there too, 'cos the Boss would put damp corn on top of the hay; you'd be surprised how quick it would dry out!

You'd cut out the hay, but you couldn't work there for long; it would be *hot!* You'd get out, and your mate, it'd be Stanley as often as not, would get in. He'd take the hay out with a long-handled pick. It wasn't a deep hole, but he'd stand and he'd spread the hay along the top of the rick. You wouldn't throw it away or elsewhere. You'd have to work quick because of the heat, and we'd be wearing hobnail boots!

They were good leather boots. The bit at the back was the 'coo' and the 'plate' was for the front; you'd put these on yourself. We'd wear stiff leather leggings; they had a strap on them and they'd cover your shins in the winter-time. We'd wear breeches too in the winter-time. They were 'all the go' then: breeches and leggings, but I preferred to wear trousers in the summer; they were cooler.'

'You'd go around one or two days before with a scythe and would cut an area wide enough for the binder with the horses, so they didn't trample the corn.

One man would cut it and about an hour later another would come round and tie it up. It had to be about an hour later because the scythe could easily cut somebody and the cutter could do it without worrying.

This is the Boss [see photo below]; I can see it is, with his trilby hat on. He's on a binder with three horses; it was a clever machine in them days. We used a binder for corn harvesting.

When the binder was moved on the road, by horse, it would have two wheels then. When it went into the field, you'd take these two off and the machine would drop onto the ground and rest onto the big wheel which done the work.

Usually, you would use three horses, all the time, when you were cutting corn with a binder, because it was a *heavy* machine. He might have had just two for the photograph, or perhaps he was moving it into another field...

If the land *was* steep and the horses were pulling a heavy load, like a binder, we'd use a fourth horse, a fore-horse, in front of the other three: to help the others. It would be put in front to help pull them up the hill. The three would all be strapped together, so there'd be one man looking after the fore-horse and another man, the driver of the machinery, could stay on his seat. When we needed a fore-horse, it could be any of the horses.

Going downhill, it would be cutting it, once you'd cut an area a good width around and up the steep edge. You'd put it out of gear to go up if it was very steep and back in gear when it was at the bottom of the field or coming downhill; the gears acted like a brake.

While the three horses were going around pulling the binder, you let the man with the fore-horse walk back to the bottom of the hill to restart. By the time the three-horse team had returned to the bottom he'd be there to help them up again. The three in the machine had the easier job.

As it went along, it would drop the corn on to the bed, then it went up a canvas and as it went down the other side it was tied. Then it was thrown out in

Fred Richards with binder and horses.

bundles to one side. As it went along, the bundles would be all in a row. There'd be rows, half-a-dozen rows, before we stacked the sheaves up.

Often as not, the horse nearest the corn would be pulling, trying to eat it as he was going round, so he was moved to the other side of the team. Prince particularly liked doing this. He was a good horse to work with mind, but he *was* a *devil!* The corn would be about three to four feet tall and he'd yank it up, roots an' all and carry it along with him, but he couldn't eat it straight off, so he'd be swinging it! I can see him now!

The corn swinging in front used to annoy the next one, so perhaps he'd try and get some! As soon as we saw what was happening we'd change them around. He was put in the middle or on the other side then. Any young horses would be moved into one position and then another, so they couldn't get used to one particular place.

You couldn't start harvesting the corn until after dinner, between 1pm and 2pm, because it would be too damp with the dew after breakfast. The farm workers would start in the afternoon and the extra help would help after they'd done a day's work. It wouldn't dry straight away; it had to be stoked up. Naturally, the bottom part of it would still be green. You couldn't knock it about too much either; else you'd knock the seeds out of it.

When you go round past the seaside and the car park in Combe Martin, behind the field with the coat of arms, there's a steep field; we called it Evidence Field. It didn't belong to my Boss, but his eldest married the daughter of West Challacombe Farm: Frances Wyborn; it belonged to them. I used to go and help out here sometimes.

We had to have a long pole to put on the cart, when we were loading it with sheaves of corn up here because of the steepness. It would fall over easy on a steep field if it wasn't loaded properly. The pole kept the cart upright; you'd put your weight on the pole and you'd load on top of the pole. Our weight on the pole and the weight of the corn would keep the cart from toppling over. You'd push it under the load and keep it there. You could take it out when it was loaded properly: no fear of it tipping over then.

You wouldn't load it completely until you were on your way out. You'd collect some sheaves on the way out of the field and that would finish the load. It wasn't all beer and skittles you know!

When the stooks'd dried out, then you'd load it. When the field was full of sheaves, the men would gather these up, stack them up into six small bundles, with their heads together and leave it to dry out for a few days. You'd work until nine or ten at night, but you had to stop before the dew started to fall again. It had to be 'bone dry', otherwise it would go mouldy and then it wouldn't go through the threshing machine.

After the corn was cut, there'd be corn on the ground and the pigs would go out and eat it up. Once, we had about eight pigs that used to run around and they were found in a corn rick eating the corn! They'd sleep under the corn rick when they could!

It seems cruel, but you had to get rid of the rats otherwise they'd eat the corn. They'd nest underneath the ricks. A rat-catcher would be expensive to use. We would buy poison and put it on bread to catch them and we'd use gin-traps, but we'd go around the round ricks with wire netting, which we'd put be a few feet [approx. 90cms] away.

We'd put a couple of farm terriers in this space, on a nice moonlit night. We'd have a pick and rock the ricks. We'd rock it towards the top: it would be lighter at the top. We'd shake it and the rats'd be disturbed. They'd try to run out, but they couldn't escape because the wire was small-holed.

The dogs would catch them in the right place at the back of the neck. If they caught them by the tail they'd have a chance to bite the dog. We'd have a few in the hay ricks but not as many as in the corn ricks; there was plenty to eat here!

'We had to walk them for the grass or the market.'

When it was summer and 'ot, sometimes we started work at 5.30am or 6.30am in the morning, if we needed to move bullocks or sheep. We moved them early, 'cos it was cooler.

I used to get overtime money to get there early to take or move the sheep or bullocks along the roads: five or six miles. We'd move them to a different field; the Boss rented grass in different places.

We took them to Hewish Barton, on the Barnstaple to Ilfracombe road.[139] The Boss would go ahead in his car to warn people that cattle were behind, but there was a lot less traffic *and* it was slower. We'd walk them on light nights too. We'd be too busy during the day! We'd move them and leave them for a few weeks.

We'd move ewes and lambs as well for the grass. You had to have a good dog with you. The lambs wouldn't be newly-born, but if the lambs went the wrong way you couldn't send a dog; they'd be too

---

139 This farm is in Bittadon, a village approximately 6 miles from Home Barton.

THE BOOK OF BERRYNARBOR

Cattle on the move in Braunton c.1920s-1930s.

Moving sheep through Combe Martin by The Old Custom House c.1900.

frightened and that would make it worse. They'd come back eventually; you had to have patience. Sometimes, we'd have twenty to thirty sheep to move; we'd walk them.

We'd move seven or eight for market. You'd put them in a cart, same cart to move the hay on the farm. They had sides, rails, but hurdles[140] had to be added to make it higher, so the sheep couldn't jump out. If there were seven or eight packed in they couldn't jump and they were enough for a horse to pull to Barnstaple Market.

We'd make a slope to lead them up – it was anything: could be an old door. We'd make sure that we were in a narrow section of a field, a farmyard or lane so they couldn't get past. When we'd led them up, we'd use the lades front and back to keep the sheep in; the lades were higher than the sheep.

When we took the sheep to market, we'd keep the best! While they were still lambing you'd keep them. The young ones that had arrived the previous year were called hogs,[141] about a year old, just lamb size.

We could tell the sheep by their teeth too. We called them two-tooths, or young hogs. When they were older, we called them four-tooths, then six-tooths or full-mouths and we'd keep all of these, but there were nowhere near as many sheep then as there are today.

When they were losing their teeth, like old people, they'd be called broken mouths and we'd get rid of them! They couldn't eat so much so they weren't getting fatter!

When we took bullocks through Combe Martin we had to keep them moving; they could look at the shop windows and see their reflections and *could charge*.

We went from Barton Farm to East Challacombe Farm too; West Challacombe Lane is before the Pack of Cards[142] and there weren't many bungalows along there then; it's a long steep hill. You can get to Hangman Hill from here. You could go along Shute

The Pack of Cards c.1920s. Harvey Barton, Bristol
Perhaps Combe Martin's most famous landmark and public house.

---

140 A hurdle was a temporary fence made with interlaced sticks, often from willow trees.
141 The Devon name was 'hugs.'
142 A Grade II listed public house, built in about 1700 to resemble a deck of cards, with, reputedly, winnings from a card game. Built on a plot measuring 52' x 52', it has 4 floors, 13 doors, 13 fireplaces and, pre window-tax, its window panes were equal to the number of numbered cards in a pack.

Lane and on to East Challacombe if you didn't want to use West Challacombe Lane. The farmers didn't mind if you used their fields as long as you shut the gate; you could go through with a horse and cart and cut through. You could go to West Challacombe first, then East.

When we took the animals to the fields at East Challacombe we always had a dog with us. We had several over the years. We always had one for the sheep and one for the bullocks.

It wasn't worth having a transporter for a few miles. We knew the short cuts; we were used to walking in them days. There wasn't much traffic either.

There were no *large* transporters then; we *had* to walk them for the grass or the market. You couldn't rush them; they'd get 'ot. There used to be a couple of big fields near Blackmoor Gate[143] and we'd take them the night before; they were safe in the field. They'd be sold the next morning.

Some farmers would put a few on a horse cart and take them to market that way, but we didn't. The markets weren't just at Barnstaple. There was a market near the station at Mortehoe and at Blackmoor Gate; there's still regular sales at Blackmoor.

We'd ring up Watts Transport, in Braunton... South Street, for a transporter. They'd come the next day. It'd take about eight good-sized bullocks for market.'

'When it was 'ot, the sheep would sleep in the shade and at blackberry time, the bluebottles or blowflies would eat the berries and then drop onto the sheep and lay their eggs. The maggots would get into the sheep and eat their skin.

Remember, they'd be out in *all* weathers, so you dipped them *twice* a year. The blowflies would avoid them for a while, but the dip would go. The flies would go for their dirty parts: their feet and their behinds.

Sheep-dipping was done in a large cement bath, owned by the large farms. Not every farm had a bath but we did. The farms that didn't had to drive their sheep to their nearest bath. Hurdles were used to keep the sheep in rows. They were tipped in to the dip to prevent flies from hatching their eggs in the sheep and then they were hooked out and walked or ran up the slope.

It was hard work. You'd pick them up; their backs were against you and their back legs would go in the bath first, then their behinds. Then you'd turn them over on to their fronts and you'd be standing over them. You'd push them in this 'water' a couple of times and you'd have a hooked stick, with a double hook on it, made for the job, to push them down by their backs and hook them up by their necks.

I've had policemen watching us on Barton Farm. I expect they went to other places as well. They didn't know the first thing about dipping, but the Boss would be there as well. I suppose it was part of their job to be there.'

South Street, Braunton c.1938.
© Photograph from the Tom Bartlett Collection, EX34 9SE

Watts livestock transport lorry being unloaded at Barnstaple's cattle market in the 1960s.

---

143 Blackmoor Gate is on Exmoor's edge and '6.8' miles from the village.

Chapter 6

Animal Actions

'On Barton and other farms, they used to do fox-hunting. Then, meat from cows that had died would be used for the hounds. If a cow died, you'd ring Tellams[144] in Barnstaple: a firm that used to do that sort of job. If a cow or horse was old, they'd come over with a hand gun, put it to their heads and death was instant. If a cow died in the sheds, it was difficult to get him out because their legs would get in the way. The door surrounds had to be taken off to help!

They'd come with a lorry and they'd have a rope on a pulley, a hand wind. The tailgate would act like a ramp and the driver would wind it up and drag the cow across the ground. It was a heavy job to wind it in, up the ramp and into the lorry. They wouldn't just come out for yours; they'd go off and get others, so the first one to load was the easiest.

Anyone could join in the hunt if their horse would jump over the fences. A lorry would bring the hounds and once the hunt was over, the lorry would come to collect them.

Sometimes there would be a couple that were missing. They knew how many they'd dropped off but some dogs stayed in the fields overnight. As soon as you saw them you'd ring up the Master of the Hounds and somebody would come along with a van or a car to collect the few!

**'he'd run over the backs of sheep
to go beyond a flock.'**

The farm dogs were only trained by the Boss. They were good dogs, but I think the dogs are better trained today. They're trained by sheepdog trainers now. You'd get a young dog, just learning, with a collar on and you'd tie this dog to an older dog and they'd have to go together. The young'un would learn; it'd gradually come to it.

Shep was creamy yellow in colour; he was a real good dog for the bullocks. If a bullock went down a side road he would get him back. You had to have a rougher, an aggressive dog, for the bullocks: one that would go in front of them, one that would have the sense to turn them.

If you came to a junction and you wanted them to go ahead, you'd say, "Go by", wave your hand and he'd go and stand by the other lane and the bullocks would continue. He'd be ready to snap at their noses to make them turn round if they were going the wrong way. They would be running with their heads down; they had horns then and could be dangerous, but he'd turn them. When they turned, he'd grab the end of their tail to hurry them on a bit!

Rose was a sheep dog. She was clever and a good dog on the road. If she couldn't get through and past the sheep, she'd nip over a hedge, through a field and beyond them to get ahead and make them turn around: about fifty or sixty or more.

Ben was another: a black and white collie. He'd run over the backs of sheep to go beyond a flock. The sheep would run together and keep together in a lane, so he had to go over their backs!

If you wanted one particular sheep you'd show it to him. Perhaps it was a bit lame; he'd hold it the best he could. He'd trip it over and grab it by the throat; there'd be thick wool there. If it got away, you'd know which one it was; he'd be running after it!

He'd bring the geese in as well. If they were around the farm implements, at nights, he'd go round the rick yard and find them and bring them into their sheds. You'd stand in the shed and he'd bring them in to you.

He was a good dog. If the sheep were up at Napps, he'd go and collect them. The Boss would tell him to "Go round." The Boss couldn't see them and the dog couldn't see the Boss over the hills; the sheep'd be a couple of fields away, but he'd bring

---

144 Tellam & Co Ltd, Derby Road, were 'licensed horse slaughterers'. Their premises included other sites in Hatherleigh, Newton Abbot and Tiverton. Today, Tellams Incineration near Exeter tests and disposes of 'Fallen Stock'.

117

Man, sheep and dog...

them back to the gate and the Boss would count them through.

If there were some missing, he'd send the dog back again. If a sheep was caught in brambles or it was dead, he'd stand where he could see the Boss and he'd bark, so he knew something was wrong. He's very like the soft toy that sits with me today. Wherever I went, he would come and find me and lie down wherever I was working.

'She kicked and broke the frame'

To prepare the horses for work, you had to feed them well, so their breakfast: the black oats or the white, chaff and mangels went into their mangers. The corn would always liven them up a bit. They never ate what they'd slept on. They'd eat the corn and that at breakfast, lunch and for their dinner.

We'd go into the loft and pull the hay down and fill

their racks, over the mangers, so they could eat it when they wanted. The hay was there as an extra for them. We put their food in the mangers, while they were drinking. In the winter time, the horses were 'laying-in'. They would have the corn etc, but they wouldn't have so much of this because they weren't working.

We had a hutch at the back of the stables with a lid over it. It would be filled with corn. This wouldn't be ground down, but they weren't supposed to eat too much. Once, Tidy managed to get her halter off, so she could lift up the hutch lid. She kept her head in and fed. She wasn't one of the ploughing team; she was one of the odd ones that pulled the carts. When we discovered what she was doing we put a stop to it and put a latch on to it to stop her!

The odd horses would be kept outside, unless it was a very bad night. They wouldn't be covered with blankets; they'd have to rough it! First thing we'd do, if we brought one in from the field was to groom it; we looked after the ones inside and out. You'd use an odd horse to pull farm carts to collect hay and straw or the butts to collect the mangels and turnips.

Duchess was a real terror. She could be nasty and upset the others. She *used to kick*. She was a good worker, but some days she'd kick real hard and one day she broke the wooden draught, so the Boss said, "Right, we'll get metal ones." She didn't like the chains touching her, when they turned they would rub against her. If she caught her leg over the chain it used to set her going; she'd *kick and kick*. She was always better with another horse, but there were days when you had to work her on her own.

Sometimes, she had to pull a stone roller – rolling the grass seed. She'd have to go steady, so we didn't use her too much for this! We'd use Tidy; she was a lovely mare – quiet, no problem. One day I was with Duchess that had a roller in a wooden frame. She kicked and broke the frame, so the roller rolled down the hill. Thankfully, I stood out of the way. It rolled into another farmer's field. I had to go right down to the bottom of the field and pull it back! Duchess didn't have any foals, because the boss knew what she was like. He didn't want another one like her!

'they'd walk back to their stables'

If you were out in the fields, there weren't toilets nearby! You'd pick a bunch of grass or a dock leaf to clean yourself. Sometimes there'd be a stinging nettle in with the dock; that'd make you jump! You'd have to use a hedge. When you were ploughing with the horses, you couldn't leave them, especially a young one.

You had to hold the horse, undo your buttons: your fly. There was always six buttons; then there was your braces, wide braces to go over your shoulders, then a belt as well. You just had to get on with what was necessary! Sometimes if you were working in the field with somebody else, you could call them over so you could go off to another field...

The team were the specials, the best: two good ones who were 'willing to go'. They'd be in the stables, bedded down on a bed of straw, which would be about two foot [60cms] deep. These were the ones that were used for the ploughing, harrowing and cutting grass, but if two were doing the ploughing, you'd get another to do the harrowing.

Their dirty bedding, the straw, was cleared out daily and replaced with clean. The fresh was put on top and the dirty stuff was put under their manger. They'd lay on the clean stuff and when it was *really* dirty it was put outside. If you left it long enough it would rot down. Horse manure is the best there is!

We cleaned out their stables and sheds *everyday* and put their manure in a big pile in the yard. As long as the horses could stand up, the ground not slippery in any way, the odd horses would take it in the farm butts to the fields.

We would close the yard gate and let them have a good drink from the trough and then they'd walk back into their stables. The trough in the yard was always kept clean; they wouldn't drink any rubbish. The water tap was in the trough and the water came from our wells on the farm.

On a wet and mucky night, after a day's work, after you'd been ploughing, you'd bring two horses down to the seaside [Combe Martin]. You'd ride one and hold one. You'd back them in to the water if they didn't like it and walk them up and down in the seawater. It was good for their hooves... to keep them clean. You'd dry their legs off with straw.

'sometimes you had a job to hold them'

You had to clean the horses' harnesses and polish their brasses over the weekend; this was a winter job: when they were in their stables. They had to be cleaned in your time and not the Boss's.

When Stan was the Horseman, he'd come over on a Sunday morning and use Brasso; he'd go in the house and ask the Missus for it. The brasses were polished on a Sunday so that they were smart for the working week; you'd take pride in the horses. Stan would sit in the stable for hours with the horses. We *really* looked after them. We'd sit in their stables, on the box that had the corn in, and polish. There'd be one horse, Tidy, she'd almost be talking to you; she'd nuzzle you and neigh when you were in her stall.

When the horses were in the fields we could see the brasses shining across the fields from Combe Martin. It wouldn't be every farmer or Horseman that would bother, but it were lovely to see.

Horse brasses.

ANIMAL ACTIONS

Fred Richards was very particular and we all took great care of everything. He'd go to Barnstaple on a Friday, to a shop where you could get anything for a horse. He'd buy the oily black polish from here. On a Monday morning you'd polish their hooves.

It was a Horseman's job to use paraffin all over their backs in the summer too 'cos there were big horse flies around and they'd upset the horses so much that sometimes you had a job to hold them! It made their backs shiny and it kept the flies away, but when they got hot and sweaty it didn't work so well.

Muck and earth would get into their hooves and stayed if you didn't clean them out properly; they'd get what we call 'thrush' and it would smell *terrible*. If you were interested in them, you'd look after them and they'd look after you.

In them days, you didn't keep a stallion in the same field. A man used to come round with a stallion, when they knew the time was right. I don't know where he was from, but he'd just come round; he knew which farms to visit, but his stallion would have to do his farm work as well.

Usually, the young horses would go to a horse-breaker before they worked on a farm. The horse-breaker wasn't in Berrynarbor, so the colts would be sent away. They had to get used to working with chains and going in a cart or with a butt. When they came back you'd have to get them used to working with an older horse. You wouldn't put two young ones together. Sometimes they would upset the older horses.

If you looked at a horse's teeth you could tell their age. The saying of: 'Never look a gift-horse in the mouth' meant that it probably wouldn't be any good!

Sometimes, I used to walk up to Barton on a Sunday afternoon. I'd go for a ride on Star. She was on the farm when I went there. It wasn't a pleasure really, because she'd always want to be off. She liked to be going fast!

She had a white star here [between her eyes]. She wasn't a big pony by no means and she didn't like the main roads or the double-decker buses *at all*! You had a job to hold her tight on the main roads.

She was used to working on the moor. The boss had bought her from Blackmoor Gate. She was good for him!

She was knowledgeable; she'd looked after the bullocks on the moor; she knew where to find them. If she heard one of ours mooing, you'd hold her and she'd go back for it. When they'd got the cows together, she'd bite their tails to keep them moving.

You'd saddle her up in the mornings; you'd get her ready. If anybody rang you'd use her to go out and check on a cow or a sheep and you'd go right away. You'd put her bridle on and the dog would be under the manger, laying in front of the pony ready to go. She'd be already to go.'

◊ ◊ ◊

Chapter 7

Time Out

As a farm labourer, it is logical that Ron's working week would be devoted to all-things agricultural; however, like his educational days, there were occasions when he participated in other activities instead, before or after his hours at Home Barton. The majority of his working years were spent here, but time was spent elsewhere too.

His 'activities' were, at times, affected and directed by others, near and far. Memories of some incurred capital revelations.

'Fred's eldest son, Brian, married and moved to Fairview[145], on the road to West Down; he didn't have anybody to work for him. I was asked to help. I stayed here for about five years.

I had a visit from the Boss – out of the blue. He said, "Ron, you've got to come back to Barton Farm, 'cos the Missus wants you. Brian will have to get somebody else."

It was easier work here than on Barton; it was flatter! I was quite happy working for Brian but the Boss said I was needed, so I went.

I used to help the Missus with many chores: collecting logs and coal for the fires, lighting the fires, sawing up small logs for the boiler, for wash days, which were *always* on a Monday. The only way to dry clothes then was outside, so ironing would probably be done a few days later in the same week. She used to say, "We haven't got any eggs Ron." So I'd go out in a nearby field; they could be anywhere...

'The rabbits were clever...'

When I was still living in, the Richards' boys and me used to go out with a torch, a good strong torch on some dry nights and the light would dazzle the rabbits and then they would *just sit*. They wouldn't know which way to go; you wouldn't make *any* noise. You could pick them up, hold their back legs and you'd pull their head quickly: death was quick.

You'd take them into the farmhouse, take off the head and legs and then skin it. If you knew the right thing to do you could pull it off in one go and the meat would go in a pie or a casserole. In them days you knew the rabbits were all right: no myxomatosis[146] then!

The men in the village would do it too, mainly on a Saturday afternoon, a Bank Holiday or on Boxing Day. They'd go to the farms and the farmer would be glad to get rid of the rabbits. Most everywhere they'd do it! The men'd put a net over the holes before they started, but the rabbits were clever; they'd make a bolt hole in the grass; they'd already got that done!

You could put a ferret, a line ferret in. You'd put a string over its mouth so it couldn't bite the rabbit and taste the blood; if he started to eat it, he'd stay there! Sometimes a man would hold a piece of string, a line, tied to a small collar around its neck. Some would put a bell on its collar, so they could hear them, but most times, the men would have a good dog with them. Most ferrets are very good; if there's nothing there, they'd come out. The ferret would chase it out and the dogs would catch them.

Some would have a net and a good dog; others would just use a gun. If they hadn't got a gun, they'd have a dog.

It could be a dangerous thing to do, rabbiting, 'cos they'd have double-barrelled shot guns with cartridges; you could have one man one side of a hedge and one the other. I was told that Revered Churchill's brother was shot on a Saturday afternoon rabbiting. There was a big field behind Birdswell Cottages and he was near a hedge waiting for the rabbits. There was a metal fenced-off area. It was in memory to him...' I haven't seen it for a while so it must have rusted away.

You wouldn't throw the skins away! You'd keep them. The gypsies would come round and shout, "Rags, bones or rabbit skins". What they did with the

---

145 Fairview Farm is now another holiday location; their 'stone and cob farm cottages are next to the farmhouse.'
146 Myxomatosis: a contagious, usually fatal rabbit disease. In the 50s, it was introduced to the UK to reduce their numbers.

Rabbiting – a game plan! There are nearly 40 rabbits here.

skins, I don't know.[147] They used to come round door-to-door too selling wooden, handmade clothes pegs and other odds and ends and they'd tell your fortune.

They used to take their horses out of their caravans and they'd put them in anyone's field: the nearest one when it was getting dark. They'd put their caravan by the hedge, not many cars around then so it would be on the road. You wouldn't argue with them; they'd be strangers and *they could be funny*.

A rabbit-catcher would come from Combe Martin to the farms too. He'd set about two or three hundred traps on ours. He'd set them one side of the road, and then he'd do the other side: Napps fields.

When the traps were new, they would be soaked in water, so the rabbits couldn't smell them. They had a 'new' smell. You had to cover them with earth, grass and a few leaves so they didn't see them.

When the trapper had finished on ours he'd go to another farm. When the traps were to be collected they were put in piles of fifties by the trapper and then it was always the next farm's job to send somebody to collect them.

When they were caught, he'd bring them all in to the farm and a man with a lorry would collect them and take them to the train stations: Ilfracombe, Barnstaple, Mortehoe or Blackmoor Gate, whichever was the nearest to his last collection.[148]

'You had to make sure they were completely dry'

When the season was over, the manure used and the seeds sown, we'd have about two hundred sacks. *Everything* was delivered in sacks. The sacks would be *big*; they'd have coal in 100cwt sacks; manure'd be 2cwt and there'd be 1¼cwt of cow cake and *you'd* lift 'em! The sacks would always be good strong sacks, hessian: sackcloth.

---

147 Rabbit skins were sold; the fur was removed and used by furriers to stuff beds, sofas and pillows; their skins were used to line jackets and cloaks or used by hatters.
148 Managed by 'First Great Western', Barnstaple is part of 'The Tarka Line', with trains travelling to Exeter. 'Mortehoe and Woolacombe' station opened, in 1874, one of the 'Barnstaple to Ilfracombe Railway' stations. This company was a subsidiary of the 'London and South Western Railway.' The station closed in 1970 and remained derelict for many years, but is under development for housing currently. Southern Railway purchased the 19 miles of the 'Lynton and Barnstaple Railway' in 1923, but this line was closed in 1935. It had three stations: Lynton, Woody Bay and Blackmoor Gate. Rolling stock and track were sold off, but since the 70s, thanks to volunteers, a two-mile round trip on a narrow-gauge steam locomotive is possible from Woody Bay. Refreshments are still possible too as one of the old station buildings became The Old Station House Inn at Blackmoor Gate.

Ilfracombe Railway Station. The Clifton cinema poster on this station dates this photograph as it began operating in June 1964. Previously, it had been the Gaumont and prior to this it was the Scala that Ron has spoken of and visited.

Taxis waiting for passengers alighting at Braunton c.1910. The Barnstaple to Ilfracombe line called at Braunton Station.

TIME OUT

Braunton Railway Station. Braunton was the largest station on this line. This land is covered, mainly, by a sizeable car park, but two original station buildings remain: the Station Master's house is now a newsagent's and the goods shed is occupied by the Museum of British Surfing. On its perimeter are also: The Countryside Centre, a youth centre, police station, medical centre and a pharmacy. The station ceased to operate in 1970.

Lynton & Barnstaple Railway. Chuffing its way across the Exmoor countryside; a card posted in 1926.

We used to take them down to the stream, opposite the saw mill, near the meadow on the left-hand side, near the bus stop. This was 'Pond Meadow' and we'd wash them all. Two of us would do it.

We didn't have rubber boots when I first started on the farm; we all had nailed boots. Then the Boss bought a pair of rubber boots for himself. He was paddling about in the stream one day and he said, "You boys ought to get yourselves a pair of *these*!"

We'd take a door down there, a decent one, from off an empty shed, and a broom. We'd take it to a shallow part of the stream, to protect your feet and to wash the sack. The sack would be on the door, in a few inches of water.

One of us would use the broom, stand on the door and brush the sacks clean. Then he had to put his hand into the wet sack to turn it inside out to clean this side. The other one would pass the sacks to the man in the water and then they'd be passed back to him to dry for a bit on the nearby bushes. We'd take it in turns.

When they were washed, you'd load them onto the cart, so it gave the horse something to do. They were heavy when they were wet; to take perhaps two hundred quality wet sacks on the cart was a heavy load for the horse. They were taken up the Old Coast Road to the farm.

When you got to the farm, you had to hang them up on good strong ropes, around the rick yard in the sun. You had to make sure they were completely dry, otherwise there'd be mildew. Then we'd roll them up, perhaps twelve at a time and they'd be hung up from a beam in the granary so they'd be off the ground: so that no mice or rats could get to them. One hole and they'd be *useless*.

'the horse was pulling the rope down'

Dick Richards' son, Bill, worked for his father and he had a lorry. He used to collect bricks or cement from Barnstaple, from the builder's merchants. They would be brought back in the evenings mainly, to his father's yard, which was near Richards T.V, in Combe Martin. I used to go with the horse and a farm butt the next day.

I'd be off the farm for the day. It was nice to get away for a bit; it made a change. I'd be told by the Boss to go and help. I used to go to the yard and collect the bricks or cement and take it closer to wherever they were needed: the site. This was the only time we'd take food with us, for us and the horse. When we had filled the cart with building materials, we'd take off their head collar and the bit so they could eat.

The lorries had arms to collect and deliver the loads. When the building was going up, with pulleys and blocks, the horse was pulling the rope down or outward and the man with a barrow on a plank would be going up with the bricks or the mixed cement. This was in Combe Martin mainly.

The fuel for fires and the ranges was shipped across the Channel, from South Wales, and we collected it. *Snowflake*, the coal vessel, delivered... about two or three times a year: once the coal was in the cellars it could be there for months. It was delivered on the light mornings and light evenings; it had to be daylight so you could see and it would come in on a high tide. We'd be at the beach about 5.30pm or 6.00pm in the morning.

Her captain, Captain Sydney Irwin, was a Combe Martin man. There'd be about half-a-dozen of us from different farms with their farm butts and some workers from Combe Martin would come with theirs. We had to go to the water's edge to fill the butts, the dung butts, and then the horses had to take the coal to the depot in Combe Martin. The horses didn't like working in the sea, so you had to back them in so they couldn't see the water. They used to stand in about a foot of it.

To load the coal, the men from the ship, the Captain and his son, would put the coal in the hampers or the mawns.[149] They would be in the ship, using spades to fill them. A pulley was used to bring the hampers or mawns up to the side of the ship and to pull them out of the boat.

Four or five loads were needed to fill a butt. You had to hold the horses for the first load, because the noise of the coal falling into the butts would frighten them.

You had to work hard; you couldn't waste time because of the tide. We had to push the butts tight to the side of the ship so no coal was spilled; you had to be careful otherwise you'd get black looks from the Captain and his son. If you dropped any, it would be washed away by the sea. We took the coal to Mr and Mrs Laramy's yard in Cross Street; I think this was where the new museum is now.[150]

While the tide was out we'd have to work quick; the ship *had* to be emptied! We'd be finished by the afternoon.

The same horses that took the coal were then taken back to the farm and would work again, but you'd give them an hour's break, take them back to the farm and put them in the stable for a feed. You

---

149 'Mawns' are two-handled wicker baskets. In Clovelly these were used for transporting herrings.
150 The coal yard was the museum's ground floor.

◇ TIME OUT ◇

Snowflake *coming into Combe Martin*.

Snowflake *in Combe Martin Bay*.

Strawberry picking at Silverdale, 1919.

could have something to eat yourself and then you'd start work again on the farm. In the summer they could also work doing the hay harvest in the evening. We used to take a load of coal home to the farm 'cos this fuelled the threshing machine.

We would take our sandwiches with us, but you couldn't stop to eat them. You'd set out your sandwiches alongside others and when you were left with an empty butt, near lunchtime, Mrs Laramy would know which was yours and she'd come across holding your sandwich for you to have a bite. You'd empty the butts into the yard and then finish your lunch. To fill the hold for their journey home, they'd wash it out and fill it with Combe Martin strawberries[151] to be taken back to Wales.

William Laramy had two brothers working for him: Fred and Charlie Wilcox. They'd fill the hundredweight bags and the horses delivered all around the villages, Berrynarbor, Combe Martin, Arlington and East Down. They had a round every week and they'd ask you if you wanted coal; if you didn't they'd go on to the next house. They'd have ten or twelve bags of 1cwt each. *That* was a heavy load for a horse! They delivered along the flat bit first, at the bottom of Pitt Hill, and still have half a load, they'd go up to Goosewell and the load would be lighter.

'They were easier to catch than the farm horses.'

Fred and Emma used to travel up by train to stay with relatives. I think they went up by train anyway, but they had cars on the farm. 'They were away for about two weeks; this was their holiday. The Boss could leave the farm; Stan knew exactly what to do.

They bought *horses* in *London*, probably, because they were cheap. He bought them to sell on to other farmers and made a bob or two. In London, they would have been the ones that had pulled handcarts, milk carts and funeral carts. When they were in London, they went to the Elephant and Castle[152] to buy half a dozen horses.

---

151 Strawberries have been grown in Combe Martin since the 1860s and are still grown here, although the growers have declined in number. Its mild climate and steep south-facing slopes are believed to produce the 'Best in the West'. Royal Sovereign was a popular variety. They were a shilling (1/- or 5p) a punnet in Ron's day.
152 See appendices.

TIME OUT

They were put on a train to Ilfracombe. Two of us would be there to collect them and walk them home. We'd each ride one and the other four would be on leads and harnesses and follow on behind.

The ex-London horses had to be re-trained to get them used to the harness. They didn't like the chains around their stomachs or their backsides. When they were harrowing; *they'd kick.* They weren't used to holding the carts so they didn't go backwards. They weren't used to the hills and there weren't no brakes then. They were used to cars and that, but they didn't like the farm noises: us throwing the mangels or beets into the farm butts. They didn't like the mud either; they weren't used to that in the streets of London! After their training, they worked well with a farm horse; we always put them together because the farm horse knew what to do.

We never had them very long; the Boss would be keen to sell them on for a few pounds. They were easier than the farm horses to catch. They'd come to you, particularly if you were rattling cow cake in a bucket; they'd come running to you.

The farm horses *would* come, but they'd be difficult to catch. *They'd* take the cow cake and sometimes give you a kick and run off!

'we all *had* to go.'

We'd never start *any* job on a Friday; it was unlucky. You could start it on a Thursday and continue it on a Friday. The fodder for the cattle was taken out to a field on Saturdays, so that we could just open the gate and let them go to it on a Sunday.

On Sundays, only the cows were milked, mornings and afternoons, but you had to go to church after. It wasn't the day of rest, but it was an easier day. We'd be up at 7.00am.

We wouldn't use the horses on Sundays; they'd be rested, but we'd brush out the cow sheds and the yards. That had to be done *every* day.

Then we'd wash and change, dress up and go to church. The Boss or one of his older children would do the milking in the afternoon. When I was living in I'd help too; I was there for every beck and call.

We'd all go to Combe Martin Methodist Church. When I lived in, we all *had* to go. We'd pile into their car and sit on one another's knee.

We'd all go on Christmas morning too. They had a good Christmas meal and I was always invited to stay. I was treated as one of the family; the Boss treated me just like one of his own, but I used to milk the cows and then go and see my mother and stepfather.

I was working all hours when I was on the farm, but they'd always be giving me things. I was good to them; if there was anything to do, I'd do it. Many a time I used to see friends walking along the road; they used to call to me: "Leave that and come with us," but I was quite happy working... My Boss used to pay me when *I* was on holiday. It probably wasn't the full wage, but it was something...'

Chapter 8

Second World War and Married Life

*A*t the beginning of the Second World War, 1939-1945, and still living on the farm, Ron, other workers and Fred's three sons joined the LDVs: the Local Defence Volunteers, which became the Home Guard. Every Home Guard was given a specific area to protect. As Berrynarbor was small, the Home Guard was formed of men from the village, Berry Down and Combe Martin, 'but Combe Martin had its own Home Guard too.'

'When I first joined, before we had uniform, we wore armbands with LDV. The entire local group used to go to the Manor Hall for parades. Then we were given the uniform of the Home Guard: jackets, trousers, boots and caps with badges. On a Sunday afternoon, we used to go up to the Manor Hall for parades and we practised, used the gun and stood to attention. It wasn't loaded when we were up at the Hall.

The Village Hall in Combe Martin was called Kingston Hall. We used to go upstairs in the evenings, from about 7pm until 6-ish in the morning. We'd carry a rifle; it was loaded and we'd practise 'stand at ease' with the rifle [butt] on the ground. About eight or ten of us used to go. We used to parade through the village and walk by the church and down to the Rectory. I've been as far as the 'Wildlife and Dinosaur Park' on duty.[153]

Certificate, armband and badges.

---

153 This Park is 3.5 miles from Berrynarbor church.

SECOND WORLD WAR AND MARRIED LIFE

Parading by the seaside.

Two of us would go out on duty at one time and be out for two hours, to make sure everything in the village was all right. Then we would go back to the hall and two more would go out. We would walk as far as the main bay: 'the sea side.'

The last two on would be picked up by a car, beyond the seaside, and taken home. Some lived up the Sterridge Valley. The last duty would finish about 6.3am. There were a couple of cars that belonged to people on duty, so everybody was taken home. Brian Richards, one of my Bosses, could drive and had a car and he'd drive us down, when it was his turn to be on duty. Village checks were done several times a week.

I didn't go away and fight, but I still 'did my bit'. We grew extra crops, sugar beet, Swede-turnip and the flat pole cabbage to send away during the war. We grew mangels too, but we kept these for our sheep and bullocks.

When we were loading sugar beet or the Swede-turnip we had special forks for that. They had round little knobs on the end so that they wouldn't stick in to the beets. The beets were loaded and taken to Ilfracombe station and put on a train, up to London I think.

The driver would just drive, so Francis and I would go into Ilfracombe. We thought it was a lovely job: a drive into Ilfracombe; then we'd have to load the beet or the turnip on to the train.

A gorse fire occurred on Hangman Hill. We were called to put it out, because of its steepness; no fire engine could get up there, so we had to use proper beaters. The soles of our black leather boots were hot. We had to walk on the hot burnt gorse to make sure that the fire was out, but we were fortunate; all burnt boots were replaced with new ones by the Home Guard.

We were dropped at Diggers Cross on Diggers Hill and walked around a couple of big fields in Berry Down with loaded rifles, hearing planes buzzing over. Nothing happened in Berrynarbor or the surrounding area. I knew that Jerry dropped a bomb or two over Chivenor[154]; you could hear *them*. We had

---

154 Originally a civil airfield in the 30s, Chivenor opened in 1940 as a RAF Coastal Command Station. A key role was anti-submarine operations that enabled patrols in to the Bay of Biscay. 'It played an important role in the wartime battle against the U-boats in the Atlantic and the training of generations of pilots for both Coastal and Fighter Command.' '"A" Flight of 22 Squadron with two Sea King HAR3A helicopters for Search and Rescue duties' are based at what is now RMB Chivenor.

The Hangmans. John Hinde Studios

our loaded rifles, but he didn't drop around here.

We were taken by car to Berry Down to do a duty here and stayed here all evening; we'd take our sandwiches and a Thermos of tea. You go out through the village to Berry Down and turn at the sign for Blackmoor Gate [Long Lane]. Just after the turning, there was a bungalow owned by Fred Rice; he was in the Home Guard. If you were on duty here you could stay overnight.

There was no-one living here at the time. There was a bit of furniture, so we'd sleep on the sofa or the floor. Generally there were eight of us. We had to go out, two at a time, and walk for two hours at a time. It was *really* dark here: no lights, just paraffin lamps, inside the house. When we were outside, we'd collect sticks for the grate fire and take them inside, then take them home; no opportunity was wasted.

When you'd done your shift you couldn't go home; you had to stay at the Kingston Hall, not far from the seaside in Combe Martin, until everybody had done theirs. You had to get your sleep between shifts, but you didn't sleep well, there was too much joking and laughing.

We were a happy group: laughing and telling jokes – men together. There'd be some dirty jokes! There were some in them days, but not the bad language like there is today.

We'd all be taken home, about 6.00 or 6.30am. We'd get home, have a cup of tea and something to eat, put our working togs on and go to work. First job would be to go out and milk the cows. You couldn't say you were tired or didn't want to do it; you had to get on with it.

We used to go out on manoeuvres in the middle of the night, for practice. We'd be in our own homes and somebody would knock on the door, and we'd have to go. Not everybody at the same time, but 'they' – a 'big noise', perhaps a sergeant major locally, would choose who.

We had to make our way from Berry Down to the church steps in Berrynarbor without going on the road much. Sometimes we also went down as far as Sandy Cove. You could cross the roads but we had to keep off them as much as possible, so we went through fields, hedges and ditches. Most of us were Berrynarbor men, so we knew where to go and it was always on a moonlight night, so we had some light to start with. We would just be in our Home Guard uniforms. No torches were allowed. We carried loaded rifles, but we didn't have any accidents. We were out as long as it would take; get home for an hour or two before you started work.

SECOND WORLD WAR AND MARRIED LIFE

Combe Martin beach c.1890s. Pictorial Stationery Co.

Looking down Seaside Hill, Combe Martin c.1950s. G R & J Barlow

Home Guard, Berrynarbor. 'This is the young group: they were standing outside the Manor Hall.'
Back row, left to right: *Reg Huxtable, Fred Ley, Ron Toms, Fred Spear, Fred Huxtable, Gordon Newton, Alfred Leworthy, Alf Brooks, Jack Snell, Albert Osborne, Bert Kiff, Bob Lancey.* Next row, left to right: *Reg Ley, John Howells, Lewis Smith, Albert Richards, Ivor Richards, Eddie Priest, Leonard Dummett, John Vallance, Gerry Beauclerk, Dick Floyd, Percy Altree.* Next row, left to right: *Brian Richards, Stanley Harding, Parky Smith, Sidney Dummett, Colonel Newman, Albert Peachey, Claude Richards (Snr), Bob Richards, Percy Thorne, Gordon Bowen.* Bottom row, left to right: *Claude Richards (Jnr), Steve Brookman, Jim Floyd, Ken Huxtable, Lionel Dummett.*

Home Guard, 1941. 'This was the older group.' Back row left to right: *Jim Floyd, Lionel Dummett, Ned Challacombe, Frank Brookman, unknown, unknown, Denzil Draper, Bill Peachey, Alfie Brooks.* Middle row left to right: *Fourth from the left is Gerry Beauclerk: the only known figure in this row.* Front row left to right: *2nd from left is Percy Thorne, ? Osmond, unknown, Colonel Newman, Will Perrin, Arthur Snell.*

SECOND WORLD WAR AND MARRIED LIFE

Berrynarbor and Combe Martin Home Guard marching through Ilfracombe. Back row [closest to the shops], 'at the front is Sid Perrin, behind him is somebody Boyer; Bert Kiff is behind him, then I don't know, but somebody Bowden is next. I don't know the next man. Behind him it looks like Percy Altree, then it's Gerry Beauclerk. Behind him it's Dick Floyd.' Middle row: 'One of Fred Richards' sons, 'Bob Richards, is at the front. Behind him it's Fred Spear and behind him it's John somebody; he was an evacuee.' Ron was seventh in this row; Jack Snell was in front of him and Ivor Richards was behind. Front row: At the front, 'Bob's older brother Brian is on Bob's left and Claude, uncle to both marches behind Brian. Fifth from the front is Stan Harding. Behind Stan is Sidney Dummett, then it's Fred Huxtable. Behind Fred is Alfred Leworthy. Behind Alf is Francis (Frank) Huxtable and then it's Frank Brookman.

The two Claudes were uncle and nephew; Brian and Bob Richards were nephews of 'Old Claude'. The Dummetts were brothers, so were the Leys, the Floyds and the Smiths; the Huxtables were father and son. The Floyd brothers came from Lynton and Eddie Priest was an evacuee to the village, but the rest were born and bred in Berrynarbor.

'they'd always be given a hot or cold drink'

We had German prisoners of war at Home Barton, about six of them. A lorry would take them around to the farms and drop them off, half-a-dozen here and half-a-dozen to another. I think they stayed in South Molton, in a hostel. The lorry driver wasn't German and he'd do his bit at the last farm he dropped.

We had to show them what to do and work together; you couldn't tell the Boss you wouldn't. Other farms had them too, but they were always on the big farms. Some of them stayed on in the village and married local girls, but they've gone on now. They were good workers; they worked hard.

At threshing times, you'd tie your knife to your wrist so you didn't lose it. One German prisoner did this, the knife was caught by the thresher and took his hand, and it was smashed. He had to lose his hand.

When Raymond was born, at home, I had a couple of days off from the farm. When I got back, they lifted me up and carried me around, pleased for me and pleased to see me.

We had land girls on the farm too, about half a dozen of them. They would be brought in a lorry. I think they were based at South Molton too. We didn't mix with them, socially; they were only there during the day. They were good workers as well; they would do anything. They would pull out the weeds, cut hedges, cut thistles with a scythe, anything.

They used to bring their own food: sandwiches; we weren't allowed to feed them. If they were near the farm buildings they'd always be given a hot or cold drink.

A lot of men didn't come back from the war and some came back in a bad way. There were a lot of ex-servicemen who became tramps. There were rocks in Bament's Woods and they would make a cover there to sleep. They made theirself comfortable

Every Sunday, when I was at the farm, the Missus would give one a cooked dinner. He was known as 'Dr Ed'. He was a well-respected man. His sister lived in Ducky Pool Cottage. He'd been through the war and he couldn't live in a house anymore. I don't know if he was really a doctor, but he had good manners.

He'd eat his meal in the cowshed, the washhouse or sit outside if it was nice. He'd thank the Missus and then go. They'd go to other people but they knew where they were well off!

'I didn't like the smell of diesel.'

We had our first tractor, the Fordson, during the war. The younger ones were interested in those. I was a bit nervous of them. They weren't covered in then and I didn't like the smell of the diesel. I liked the horses. I was much more interested in working with them.

With a tractor you just pressed a button and unless the driver was technical they would have to call out an engineer if it went wrong. They'd pay dear for it mind, but there were plenty of engineering firms in Barnstaple and they would come out.

When we had the tractor, we had another mill. The tractor's engine had a pulley fixed to it all the time on a small wheel: a pulley wheel, a wide one. The tractor was just an ordinary Fordson. The tractor had to be in line with the mill and it had to be on level ground otherwise the belt would come off the pulley.

This mill was in the barn, fixed to the ground and was bigger than the one in the linney. There was an engine house at the side of the barn; the pulley went through the wall and was used to drive the engine. A belt would go on the pulley and we'd take the belt off when we'd finished a job. It would grind the meal, cut chaff, saw logs. We'd do these jobs on a wet day.

The engine for the big mill *had* to be wound by hand to start it. Once it had started you had to move the handle out quickly otherwise it would fly off and could hurt you!'

A (1942) 'Fordson' Tractor

◈ SECOND WORLD WAR AND MARRIED LIFE ◈

The day before his wedding day of 30th October 1943, Ron left the village to marry. They had had a holiday romance, but their marriage had been 'until death us do part', when Gladys passed away in 2001.

Wembley, now synonymous with Cup Finals, was his destination, but even a marriage had to be arranged around the farming calendar.

Their wedding vows were exchanged at Sudbury Baptist Church in Wembley and the newly-weds returned to their home on the Hill.

'Pauline Draper was one of five. Her parents lived next to what was the Parish Rooms. During the beginning of the war, Pauline had gone to London to live with her aunt and uncle and to work in a factory; I think it was a biscuit factory. Pauline and Gladys met at work. Then Pauline went to live with Gladys and her family in Wembley. They came down here on holiday and brought three other girls.

I sorted them out so to speak and picked out Gladys. I hadn't known Gladys long, but it was love at first sight, so she said yes! She was very small and only nine months younger than me. You don't think of age when you're courting, do you?

They were only here a week! They all went back to London and we wrote letters to each other; then we got married. People in the village used to say it wouldn't work or that it wouldn't last. They thought I was daft and said I didn't know what I was letting myself in for. We had our ups and downs like everyone else, but we pulled together.

We had to sow a field of winter wheat before I left the farm to get married! We all took the train from Ilfracombe to London; my stepsister Greta and my cousin Violet were bridesmaids; my best man was Bob Richards, who was about five years younger than me.

My mother and stepfather wouldn't travel to the wedding. Frank, my granddad, had died years before me granny. She came to live at 23 and was still alive when I was married. She stayed living with Mum and stepfather until she died.

We were a bit surprised when we arrived; we discovered that a bomb had dropped on the house next to Gladys's and it was a ruin. It had shaken Gladys. Her house was all shaken up too, so we couldn't stay there the night after we'd married. She hadn't told me that this had happened before I left from Ilfracombe, so it was a bit of a shock.

We stayed with friends of Gladys's in the next road for a couple of nights and we visited members of her family. Gladys's brother lived up there too, but it

The newly-weds: Mr and Mrs Ronald Francis Toms.

was a bit noisy up there, so we didn't stay there too long!

We went to live with my mother and father because we had to wait for number 16 to be empty. Mr and Mrs Will Ley of Widmouth Farm owned it and said when it was empty and if we were in the village, it was ours. They were doing me a favour. I knew them well and me mother and father knew them *very* well.

Gladys was used to having a toilet inside, because she'd lived in London. Having one outside was a bit different for her and before I went to work every morning, I had to fill a large, metal, oval-shaped bath that had two handles, with water, for Gladys to use during the day.

We had to have a bath in front of the fire too. She didn't mind even though she was used to a proper bath up in London.

We were on the Haggington Hill when the pipeline[155] work started in Watermouth. It went here

---

155 PLUTO: Pipe Line Under The Ocean. See Appendices

THE BOOK OF BERRYNARBOR

Widmouth Farm, 2012.

Widmouth Bay and the Bristol Channel, 2012.

SECOND WORLD WAR AND MARRIED LIFE

and under the sea. I could see the petrol tanks coming in, to Mill Park meadow, where the campsite is now, but I didn't see any workers.

In the mornings, I'd walk along the public footpath from Heanton Hill, down the steep-sloping field, opposite Mill Park, then along the main road to South Napps; this land belonged to Home Barton too. I had a plastic tin for my sandwiches. I carried the tin and the tea in my rucksack.

At 10, you used to have a snack, our lunch, but we'd make the tea before we left home. You'd fill a glass bottle with tea. I had two: one each side of my lunch tin. The tea was still warm at the 10 o'clock break, but by dinnertime, about 1 o'clock, it was cold when you drank it.

My granny used to knit thick socks. You'd cover the bottles with a sock before we had the Thermos flasks!

We had our snack, six sandwiches, outside in the fields or the garage or cart shed if it was very cold or wet. I had more sandwiches, another six, for dinner.

Lunch was a 'moveable feast' 'cos if the Boss wanted us to do a job, perhaps he wanted the yard cemented, so if you had a load of 'Ready Mix' delivered, you 'ad to spread it! We had wooden barrows with metal bands on the wheels, and two or three of us had to work it. *Then* we ate our lunch.

We went to the farm on Sunday mornings to feed the horses, but we didn't *work* outside on Sundays. We'd put fodder for the cows in a field and shut the gate; on Sunday mornings we just opened the gate to allow the cows to eat it. We had to milk the cows on Sunday mornings and the evenings; they were all hand-milked of course. On my day off, I didn't do this, but if somebody was sick you'd have to go in. We worked as a team.

My wife and I worshipped at the Congregational Chapel on Sundays. We were the caretakers here for about thirty years. There was a service every Sunday. In winter it was between 3 and 4.00pm and in summer on the light nights, it started at 6.30pm. I took to the chapel; I used it for quite a few years.

When Raymond was born in 1946, Gladys'd push him down into the village and then for a walk along the Old Coast Road, [behind Napps] and then round and sit on the seats by the bus shelter, opposite the saw mill and then back up to the Hill.

Before I was married I used to work six full days but after I was married I had more time off: another half day. Her parents used to come down to visit...

When the children were older we used the trains to take them away, from Ilfracombe to London. We visited their grandparents, my in-laws, and Lily, my wife's sister for a few days. We all went together, but we couldn't go at busy times.

When I wanted firewood, the Boss used to tell me

Congregational Chapel front, 2012.

Congregational chapel rear.

to go to Bament's. We could have potatoes from the big barn. You could help yourself to Swedes or turnips. You were given eggs, which was special at weekends, by the Missus. She could give you anything: fat bacon, a large piece, or pieces of pork.

They used large blocks of salt – big blocks – to cure the meats. The Missus did this. They used to put the meat in a 'salter', which was a large china container. The meat was cut into chunks and covered with salt. You had to keep moving it and checking it.

'She was always better with another horse...'

I was promoted to Horseman after I married, because Stan Harding left to work on Bodstone Farm for Mr Fred Rice. I earned more too, but I can't remember what it was.[156]

He showed me how to work the horses and how to plough. We'd put the cart near a bank and then put the tail of the cart near it. We'd run the plough onto the cart to move it to a field – they were *heavy ploughs*. He'd watch me for a while, stay for so long, and then leave you to it. When we were first learning we'd have the quieter horses, but some mornings you had to catch them!

When Stan was still working for the Boss, Francis Huxtable joined us. Before he came to us he'd worked for a builder in Combe Martin. He used to do a few odd jobs on the farm before Stanley left.

One year, Francis and I went out with a horse and cart to clear a path through the snow. We cut out the hay we wanted and by the time the cart was loaded the path was covered with snow, too deep for the horse to go through, so we cleared a bit, moved on, cleared a bit and moved on. The hooves would clog up and then they couldn't stand properly, so we *had to have* clear paths for *them*.

I worked with two of the mares mainly: Darling and Tidy, but there was Duchess, Prince and Hackley as well. Darling was the mother of quite a lot of them, but they were all there for *years* and *years*. There were always five horses and always one team of two for the main jobs of field-to-field ploughing. I used to have a team and work these to furrow the fields. There was no stopping, we just kept going, one furrow at a time. A furrow was about 6 to 9 inches deep. Once one field was finished, I, or another man, could go in and roller it with another team of horses.

We'd plough all the fields, one after the other, but you'd leave an area all around the outside, all but the bottom bit. You'd go into the field at the bottom, so you'd plough this first and then you'd keep going in the same direction, but there had to be enough space for the two horses to turn around at the sides and the top. We'd call this bit the 'forrid'.

On the plough, on the side, there was a long piece of iron, the bumper; you'd take this off when you were doing the forrid. It had a wheel, a square wheel on it. When you were doing the forrid you didn't need it and it would get in the way of doing the edge.

We'd take the horses back for lunchtime; they had to have their lunch in the stable: the trough. The Boss used to ask how you were getting on and I'd say it was OK. He'd say, "You'll get used to it." You had to be gentle with the horses. You didn't shout at them; they'd pay you back by some means.

At the end of the day, I used to take the four horses from Home Barton, along the main road to a big field called South Napps. This was only during the summer, because they'd be in stables during the winter.

It was always reckoned that if you ploughed a 1.5acre field you'd walked eighteen miles,[157] so we could do that six days a week when ploughing had to be done! A furrow was less than a foot [30cms] wide.[158]

Tractors came in on the farm during the war; it was a Fordson. We just kept one horse to take the cart or the butt out to the sheep or the bullocks, which could be loaded up with mangels. Many a time I've seen the mangels roll down the field and on to the road. The cars used to toot, as much as to say, "Careful what you're doing!"

Fred had employed a young boy, Francis Huxtable, and he worked the tractor. The plough would be trailing behind; you wouldn't be able to raise it like you could now. All the furrows had to be even; if one was higher than the other the Boss would tell you to fix the plough and do it properly.

To start with on the farm, we'd do six full days, but because Fred Richards was on the agricultural committee, he'd introduce changes first. The agricultural committee meant he'd have to go round all the other farms too and see what crops were planted and where they were planted; he was following rules...

One day he came over to me and my mate Francis Huxtable and he said you can have half-day on Saturdays, from 12 o'clock onward. This was paid holiday! This was after I was married; coo, we thought we were *really* lucky.

Fred was the first to have Ayrshires for milking cows. This was unusual, 'cos we all had the Devons.

---

156 The Agricultural Wages Act 1948 came into being 'to consolidate the Agricultural Wages (Regulation) Acts, 1924 to 1947'. When Ron first joined Home Barton, 1932, his pay, as a 16-year-old was '£1/10/9' with 'Basic Hours' of '51.1'. A local newspaper of 1965 stated that 'new rates' as from January, for 'Males 20 & over' had minimum rates of wages for workers employed in agriculture in the County of Devon'. Their weekly rate was '202/0s' (£20.2shillings 0d (pence) or £20.10p; their hourly rate was 4/6d (4 shillings & 6pence or 22.5p); their overtime rate was 6/9 (6shillings & 9pence, or 33.75p).
157 Ron, his friends and colleagues were not far out. An 'acre or 'area', an Anglo-Saxon field, was what could be ploughed by an oxen team in 1 day. Ploughing a 1-acre field equated to an 11-mile trudge.
158 'Back in the 1930s, horse and early tractor ploughs operated with furrow widths of 6 to 9in.'

SECOND WORLD WAR AND MARRIED LIFE

Other farmers came from the village to have a look at them. As far as I know he'd tell other farmers to do *this* and do *that*. He may have seen other farms with these and this gave him the idea to have them.

Home Barton was the depot for farm implements for everybody's use. People had to pay; how much I don't know and they could borrow.

'She was quicker than my pushbike!'

Fred owned or rented Smythen Farm at one time as well as Home Barton. We used to work at other farms, but most of our time was spent at Home Barton. After I was married, Frank Huxtable and I used to go down to Smythen to work. At Smythen the farmhouse was empty but the sheds were still there and the bullocks went in the fields.

Frank would go up to Barton Farm and take Star to Smythen. He lived at the old house, Sea View, on Barton Lane. I had my pushbike, but it wasn't much good. I could ride it down 'Henton' Hill, along the Lees, but we had to push a bike from the Sterridge up that steep hill to Smythen. You can get to Smythen from Berry Down. If Frank wasn't at work, I used to go up to Home Barton and take Star to Smythen. She was quicker than my push bike!

'coming and going'

When my aunt and uncle owned Miss Muffet's, they had a room at the end, near Birdswell Lane, that they used for the doctor's surgery about once or twice a week. The doctor was an Ilfracombe doctor: Doctor Bray,[159] I think. I can remember walking from Birdswell to go to the doctor's. We didn't take many tablets then, it was mainly medicine in a bottle. What pills we had were round usually: a Beecham's pill. We didn't have the different shapes like today. You didn't get tablets for everything. You had bottles of medicine and they had marks on the side for the dosage so you knew what to take.

After the war the number of buildings in the village changed here too. People were coming and going and there was lots of building going on. Where there was a large plot of land, they've built a house or bungalow.

People used to like gardening. You'd grow your own. Today, most of them seem to live on tins!

The circus used to come to the Rugby Club, Brimlands playing field,[160] Ilfracombe, but it wasn't used for rugby. I was only a young boy then; I went with me mother and father. While they were in the area, they would bring the elephants up the Haggington Hill from Combe Martin; they used to perform in a few fields above the Rectory in Combe Martin too.

Two elephants would be walked to perform in the field where the Rugby Club is now. The men driving them had a job and it must have took some time 'cos they'd stop and pull at the leaves and branches of the trees. They say it's cruel today, but they seemed to be well looked after. It wasn't just elephants; there'd be horses and clowns.

The school dumped the blackboard while I was still working and it went in a skip. I took it home; I asked... My son painted it black, but there should be a bit of green paint on the back; and it was taken to the chapel and then for the Manor Hall. Bill Bury, he had a lot to do with the Manor Hall at the time, so when the chapel closed, I had it over at my place and then I took it to him.

The storage area for chairs at the Manor Hall, the back room, was a skittle alley. This was a lean-to, the length of the Manor Hall, with a tin roof. You could get right around on the outside. Gladys and I never went. We weren't very interested or very sporty, but she belonged to the W.I. and we used to go to the pictures in Ilfracombe.

Ilfracombe High Street. With the shops and types of car that Ron would have seen in the 1950s.

---

159 This was 'Doctor Anthony Bray, M.B., Ch.B. D.R.C.O.G.' who was the 'Senior Partner' of 'one of the two General Practices, serving Ilfracombe and District'.
160 'Brimlands', as a name, no longer appears on current OS maps. 'The new 'rugger pitch' here was opened by Mr. B.G. Lampard Vachell.' October 1936.

A Christmas celebration, with Ron. Gladys and Ron were at this Christmas celebration, so this is post 1943. He is standing behind the left table and the sixth person along. Gladys is to his right-hand side. Second lady, from the front, was a 'Miss Osmond. She sold knitting things and the like on the left-hand side of the front door to the Manor Stores.' On the back table, 'the vicar wasn't the Reverend Churchill. At the end, on the right, is Bob Richards and his wife Bett. To his right, were Mr and Mrs Cooperthwaite; she was head at Berrynarbor School and taught my daughter Sheila. First lady at the right table was Vera Greenaway. Seated opposite her, with the [light-coloured] hat on, is Vera's aunt. The lady next to her with a hat on is her aunt's sister and Vera Greenaway's mother. Next to Vera is her sister. Next to Vera's sister is Mrs Lancey and next to her is Laura Draper; she had three daughters and a son. Laurel, her son, is the man standing on the [extreme] right.

We had concerts and dancing[161] in the Manor Hall. The dancing was on Saturdays and the concerts were on Thursdays. When I married, we'd go to these, but I'd go before I was married if the girl I was courting wanted to go. It'd be mainly the local people, ordinary working people. There'd be two or three a year, but they'd only be in the winter; people were so busy in the summer. We had *real* dancing: Old Time Dancing. We'd dance around the room *together*, with music. There was always a piano in the Hall.

At the concerts, pianos were always played; *they were alw*ays there. Mrs Bessie Stevens was the daughter of the blacksmith; she played the church organ for several years. She was just one of the people that could play and a man used to come from Combe Martin and played a drum. This was Mr Norman, the father of the vegetable shop owners. He had an all-together drum; he worked the drum with his foot and the cymbals were on the side. They didn't practise much, a couple of nights before perhaps. If they made a mistake, people would laugh a bit, but they'd still clap.

They didn't hire costumes or have special lights. If they were going to say something as a farmer's boy, they'd just go dressed in farming clothes. They'd wear a red handkerchief knotted around their necks

---

161 All village organisations held dances to fund raise.

SECOND WORLD WAR AND MARRIED LIFE

Another festive gathering. Considering this was taken many years ago, numerous names were remembered, but their positions were uncertain; however, Ron's son, Ray, is the 3rd child on the left in the second row. He was born in 1946, so this looks to be an early 50s party. Others present were: Richard Armstead, Julie and Paul Bowden, Philip Bowden, Marlene Bray, Alison Brown, ? Brookman, Sheila Buchan, Malcolm Chalmers, Theodore Chalmers, Shirley Charley, Ron Cook, Maureen Dummett, June Greenaway, Robin Harding, Sybil Hockridge, Gary Huxtable, Ivan Huxtable, William Huxtable, Brian Irwin, Sheila Jewell, Cheryl Layton, Denis Mitcham, Michael Mitcham, Bernard Newton, Joan Newton, Jill Oakley, Ken Richards, Linda Richards, Yvonne Richards, Jill Sidebottom, John Sidebottom, Charlie Sledmar, Bill Smith, Graham Songhurst, Gordon Stanbury, Eileen Stanbury, Francis Thorne, Linda Thorne, Williams Toms, Michael Wharburton, Larry White, Mrs Yeo and her two nephews.

at times, no collars on their shirts, and a cap, always. They'd always wear a *red* handkerchief and they'd have their sandwiches tied up in one of these too – a clean one!

They'd have a programme, but at the end of the evening, they'd ask if there was anybody else who wanted to sing or do something and people would get up. Anyone could join in. Ivy Richards would sing. She was a good singer; she used to sing 'In Her Sweet Little Alice Blue Gown.'[162] She had a good voice. No drinks were sold. You might have lemonade or a tea or coffee.

At the end of the evening Mr Norman, he had a big car, a long car, and he'd take about half-a-dozen girls home if the weather was bad, or if we didn't want to walk them home. There weren't no police around to see how many were in the car, so they'd all jump in!

---

[162] 'Alice Blue Gown' was written by American composer, Harry Tierney, in 1919, for Edith Day, the star of his Broadway musical, 'Irene'. It became Broadway's longest running show of its time, with 620 performances. The song was, probably, his best-known and had further exposure in two 'Irene' films: 1926 and 1940. The latter starred Welsh-American actor, Ray Milland and an English favourite: Dame Anna Neagle. Theodore Roosevelt's daughter, Alice Roosevelt Longworth, had worn a gown of Alice blue that had sparked a fashion trend, but the colour is still used for insignia and trims on naval vessels named after this American President.

Junior Miss Berrynarbor. Apart from concerts and parties, informal contests were held during these dances. This one occurred during the 1950s. The 'Orchades' had been playing on this particular night. At the back, the first six girls, from the left, are unknown, believed to be holiday visitors, then it is Stella Lancey and Ruby Draper, and the ninth girl is also unknown. In the front, from the left, the first girl is unknown, then it is Lorna Richards, Pat Blackmore, Shirley Blakey and Glady Toms, daughter of Violet: Ron's cousin.

Mrs Berrynarbor Contest c.1950s. Left to right are: Mrs Helena Graves, 'Mrs Berrynarbor': Mrs Sylvia Berry, Mr Fred Ward, Muriel Richards and Rita Smith. The girls are (L to R), Sonia Stoddart and Elaine Creighton.

Ron with long service certificate & mug. Presented at the 'Devon County Show, 1980 (a) Long Service Award for 40 years (to) RONALD FRANCIS TOMS'.

The 'Boss': a retired Fred Richards.

'it didn't do me any harm'

I was never happier than when I was working. I had to leave at 7 in the morning for the farm; it was about a twenty-minute walk, in rain, snow or sunshine. I'm sure it didn't do me any harm.

I retired when I was seventy; I did about thirty years for Fred, five years for Brian and about twenty for Bob.

After I left the farm, I used to garden for people in the light evenings: just for an hour. The Lodge was a private house, when I was at school. When I left the farm, the Praters owned it and I used to go gardening for them. I'd earn a bob or two; I used to enjoy it.

Hard work doesn't hurt you; it keeps your mind occupied. My wife used to be watching telly and I was out in the garden until 8 or 9 o'clock at night, when it was light. She used to say, "Are you coming in tonight or shall I bring the bed out to you?" We had fifty-eight years together and I never heard her complain. Money isn't everything; your health is your wealth.

"He who lives the longest sees the most." I've proved it, I've seen quite a lot...'

Appendices

APPENDICES A:
Bament's Wood Quarry

For Ron and Jack, this area was a workplace. It was a few paces from a 2 mile [3.5km] stretch of coastline that, since their diggings, has been designated as a Site of Special Scientific Interest (SSSI). It is probable that they were unaware that they were working with rocks that are 350 to 400 million years old. Devon is the only county to have its name applied to a geological period: the Devonian Period, known internationally in geological circles.

Bament's Wood adjoins this dramatic stretch of coastline: between Ilfracombe about 3.5 miles [5.6km] to the west and Combe Martin a little more than a mile to the east. Its rocks of sandstone, slates and mudstone are described, as 'Ilfracombe Beds'. The rocks are 'hard and do 'ring' when hit with a hammer because they were altered by heat and pressure during earth movements.

A short woodland walk from the 'Sawmill' takes you to this section of the South West Coastal Path, which hugs the rugged cliffs and beautiful bays here. The quarry working has ceased, but walkers can still view this now quiet but impressive seascape.

APPENDICES B:
The Elephant and Castle Horse Sales

In Newington, part of the borough of Southwark, a six-foot [1.83M], vivid pink, statue of an elephant surmounted by a castle stands above the entrance to a shopping centre, once voted Europe's ugliest. It has become an iconic London landmark and has renamed this area: 'the Elephant and Castle' or just 'The Elephant'. For me, it is a once-seen-never-forgotten place: the epitome of modern mayhem. A noisy intersection, its unrelenting traffic crawls and sometimes races around London's fifth most dangerous junction: six 'A' roads converge at two large roundabouts connected by a short section of the London to Portsmouth A3 road: seemingly, an incongruous location to sell horses.

It is ironic, perhaps, that Ron, a born-and-bred Devonian knew of a market held here, more than 200 miles away, but on Mondays, more than fifty years ago, his Boss, Fred Richards, bought bloodstock south of the Thames at the Elephant and Castle Horse Repository. Previously, this location had been home to several repositories, including Tattersalls, but it and others disappeared. Tattersalls transferred its sales from Newington, London to Newmarket, Suffolk.

Horses used for delivering bread, beer, coal and milk, were sold on, through this sole and remaining Repository. Most of their trade came from the dealers, but 'hunters' were bought for the provinces; 'hacks' went to the riding schools; hiring contractors bought for film commitments and Fred was, probably, one of many farmers who bought then sold.

Bridles, night rugs and shooting sticks were among other objects that exchanged hands before many adjourned to the spacious bar of the public house: 'The Elephant and Castle'. Redevelopment of this neighbourhood began in the late 50s; the pub and other buildings made way for the high-rise homes that are part of yet another but current development project.

Unbeknown to many, perhaps, buyers and sellers were continuing horsing history here, because in 1641, the constant flow of horse power resulted in a smithy, but by the 1700s this had become the public house. The 'Horse and Castle' is an unfamiliar pair, but this quadruped has been associated with this district, albeit sporadically, for almost four hundred years. No visible tribute exists to what had been a 'metropolis of the horse trade', it is as one, former, 1940s' regular put it: 'as if none of it had ever been.'

APPENDICES

Snowflake in Watermouth Harbour after striking a rock c.1931.

APPENDICES C:
S.S. *Snowflake*

Snowflake was a 'Clyde Puffer', built in 1893 and bought by James Irwin in 1897. His son, Sydney, was the Captain that Ron knew. Originally, these vessels were built to work on the Forth and Clyde Canal. Its locks determined their length: 20.3 metres (66') with a beam of 5.54 metres (16-18'); even their boilers were upright to save on length. The wheel was on top of the boiler; the Helmsman stood here, protected only by a 'canvas dodger'. In the earliest boats, the noise emitted from their steam exhaust outlet to the funnel gave them the rest of their name. Their design changed so that they could also work in estuarial waters: the shorehead types; the last of which were built in the 30s.

She brought general cargoes, from Bristol to Combe Martin, but her main cargo was coal for the Ilfracombe gas works, collected from Lydney[163], Gloucestershire and Cardiff, South Wales. Returning shipments were also organic. Combe Martin's mild climate and sunny, steep, south-facing slopes were perfect for strawberry growing. Tons of fruit, in baskets and a cleaned hold, were shipped across the Bristol Channel to Wales.

In 1936, she struck a rock off Little Hangman, dashed back to Watermouth and beached at low tide. Only her funnel and mast were visible at high tide, but after essential repairs that took a few days, she was back to work.

A.J. Smith of Bristol bought her in 1940, then she was chartered by the Government to take water to ships and isolated river camps for the British and Allied Troops in preparation for Europe's invasion. At war's end, she returned to Bristol, but was sold again, this time to trade in the Greek Islands. Her fate and whereabouts have been unknown since she was last seen in the 1960s the Mediterranean.

---

163 Lydney is a Forest of Dean town. Coal began to be extracted from this area from 1750 onwards. A list of 'Analysis of Coal shipped at Lydney between 1880-2' mentions 'Barnstaple (incl. Fremington) receiving '16,808 tons... Ilfracombe 894 tons.' Forest coal was described as 'good house coal'. Commercial extractions had ceased by the early 1960s.

APPENDICES D:
Pipe Line Under The Ocean – PLUTO

In 1941, Admiral Lord Louis Mountbatten, Chief of Combined Operations and other senior officers planning for what would become 'D-Day', knew that a sustainable fuel supply for their tankers and trucks was vital if their invasion was to be successful. Their problem was solved in early April, 1942 by Mr A.C. Hartley, the Chief Engineer for Anglo-Iranian Petroleum Corporation. He suggested that the safest means was to pump it through a continuous length of pipe laid by ship. Cable-laying technology on the seabed had existed since the 1850s.

Siemens was approached. A month later, metres of the lead 'Hais cable': Hartley-Anglo-Iranian-Siemens, were laid across the Medway and tested under high-pressure. By December, for further testing, miles of it was laid by the converted HMS Holdfast between Swansea and Watermouth Cove, near Ilfracombe. Ron saw some related activity: 'Big tanks for storing fuel were buried on Big Meadow, near to the Cove. During the testing process, Chief Engineers Hammick and Ellis reduced the need for lead, as they suggested a steel pipe could be coiled around a large floating drum. Their Hamel pipe and drum, named HMS Conundrum, became part of Operation PLUTO.

To aid secrecy, these pipes were always referred to as cables. Manufacture of these pipelines was English, mainly, but several American companies helped. By VE day, these power lines were delivering more than a million gallons between the English Channel and Normandy. This innovative 'weapon' was a well-kept secret and achieved its aim of delivering to the allied forces in Europe, in 1944 and '45.

APPENDICES E:
The Berrys, The Bassets, The Penn Curzons, their House, their Hall and the Castle: a précis of 800 years.

Ron grew up in a village that has a castle, Watermouth. Its owners needed staff for the house and grounds. He had family who worked here and knew many other villagers who were employed here. As its location is in an agricultural area, it was the largest employer of his time and its history deserves more than a footnote...

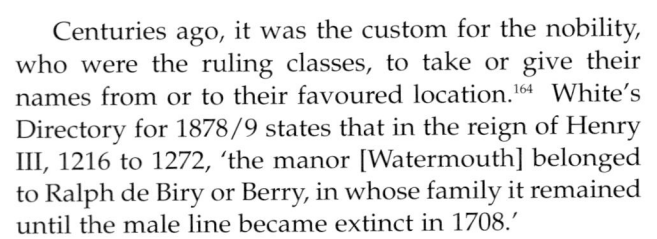

Centuries ago, it was the custom for the nobility, who were the ruling classes, to take or give their names from or to their favoured location.[164] White's Directory for 1878/9 states that in the reign of Henry III, 1216 to 1272, 'the manor [Watermouth] belonged to Ralph de Biry or Berry, in whose family it remained until the male line became extinct in 1708.'

It is believed that Ralph, a knight, and his son Richard, travelled the 20-odd miles across the Bristol Channel from South Wales to the North Devon coast by boat. This was a much shorter journey than travelling across land, furthermore, 'large areas of it [Wales] (were under) uneasy rule by Anglo-Norman barons.' It is possible that they had landed at the bay or cove, known as Watermouth Cove, which is a short walk from Berrynarbor; however before their arrival, this community had been known as 'Biria c.1150'; 'Biri' in '1167' then Bery' in '1209.'[165]

As manorial 'lords', the Berrys would have had the grandest home: a building perceived fit for a knight and his family. The village church had been here for centuries before their arrival; it bears evidence to show that this was 'almost certainly (of) Saxon origin'. It has an elevated position, and as it was traditional for manorial homes to be close to the church, and, therefore, to God, it is probable that their first home was built only paces away.

The 'Manor Hall' sign appears to name an obvious L-shaped building, but, this is the name associated with the larger and younger section: completed in 1914. The smallest and tallest part is the oldest and it is this site that is believed to be the location of their first Manor House. As the Berry family prospered and grew, it is logical to expect that this prime location was used for a larger and more luxurious home; its 'exterior was formerly ornamented with shields of arms of the Plantagenet, Bonville and other families and elaborate carved work'.

Unfortunately, all ornamentation has been removed. It could be assumed that arms relating to the reign of the Plantagenet kings, 1154 to 1399, suggest that this former family home was built during this period, but it was not. This begs a question as to why the Berry family would add their shields of arms and from others to their home.

The 'de Bonville(s)' were another noble Devonshire family, who, during the Wars of the Roses (1455-1485), had supported the House of York (the Plantagenet household) rather than the House of

---

164 'The richer and more powerful classes tended to acquire surnames earlier than the working classes and the poor. The bulk of ...surnames in countries such as England and France were formed in the 13th and 14th centuries.'

165 A Domesday entry, 1086, shows that this community was known as 'Hurtesberia' and another source comments, 'If...the DB and 12th cent forms refer to this place the original name was 'Heortes burh... burh of a man named Heort.' Burh, burgh, bery or bury are familiar place-name affixes, but they all mean the same: 'Place at the fortification' from the Old English of 'burh' meaning 'a fortified place, stronghold, fortified manor'.

APPENDICES

Manor Hall, 2012.

Lancaster. The inclusion of 'shields of arms' from both families suggests that the Berry family did too.

An architectural survey on the entire building was undertaken in 1941. The drawings include the wording: 'Judging from the design and details of the building, the Manor House was erected in late perpendicular period... about 1480... Edward IV': about five years before these 15th century English war ceased.

There cannot be many leisure and educational groups in the UK that utilise a building that is more than five hundred years old. Its first floor is known as the Men's Institute, mentioned and used by Ron and is still a male domain. Now this includes a bar and a snooker table. This is above what is known and labelled as the 'Penn Curzon Room', used by Berrynarbor pre-school.

The Berry line did become 'extinct in 1708'. Thomas Berry, a descendant of Ralph and Richard, died *without* a male heir but *with* his financial affairs in disarray: he had mortgaged his lands and property. After a lengthy lawsuit and an Order of Chancery, June 2nd 1713, legal ownership was assigned to the Basset family.

The Bassets were wealthy and property-owning, with an unbroken lineage, traceable to Thurstan Basset who had come over with William the Conqueror. He was born in 'about 1035 in Ouilly-Basset in Normandy, France' and some of his English descendants appended their names, in the 12th and 13th centuries, to the Oxfordshire and Wiltshire villages of Compton, Letcombe, Stoke and Royal Wootton Bassett.

A family tree in 'The Visitations of the County of Devon' describes this family as 'Basset of Umberleigh.'[166] During the 1400s, a John Basset had married 'Johanna, da. of Sir Thomas Beaumont'. Primogeniture, 'the right of an eldest son to succeed', had existed for centuries. John was an 'heir', but so too was Johanna. Their marriage 'brought Sherwell, Umberleigh, and Heanton Court[167] into the Basset family.'

In 1763, Eleanora Basset married John Davie of Orleigh Court, Buckland Brewer[168] and it is probable that he inherited the Basset estates on his marriage and had to adopt this surname. Their son 'Joseph' was born almost a year later, and 'assumed the name of Basset in 1803 on succeeding to the estates under

---

166 This was Umberley Manor, then Umberleigh Manor in Atherington, near the larger village of Umberleigh, approximately 20 miles from Berrynarbor. It was demolished in the 19th century.
167 Heanton Court is a landmark on the A361, in the village of Heanton Punchardon, between Braunton and Barnstaple. An impressive building, situated above the River Taw, it is now The Braunton Inn.
168 'Orleigh' is a medieval, Grade I listed building in Buckland Brewer, south-east of Bideford, 30 miles from Berrynarbor.

The Great Hall. This was 'taken in the 1890s when the Bassets were still in occupation'. Since the late 1970s the Castle has been open to the public and is also known for its 'Theme Park'; however, visitors are still able to see this 'elaborate carved work'.

his uncle's will': Colonel Francis Basset, of Heanton Court. Joseph married Mary Irwin of Barnstaple and their 'son and heir', born '14 May, bap. 30 June 1801', was Arthur Davie Basset, who would leave a lasting impression on local architecture.

The registers of St Peter's Church, Berrynarbor, reveal that some of the Bassets were married here and had children baptised here, indeed, Arthur's baptism took place here, but he was not carried from the Manor House to the church for this celebration. Censuses prove that this had ceased as a manorial home with Thomas Berry's death. Under Basset ownership, the Manor House became 'accommodation for village people.'

In 1866, Kelly's commented that the 'old manor-house (was) now converted into a farmhouse' and their Directory of 1890 reported that it 'is now in a dilapidated condition.' They were correct, because, unfortunately, in 1889, a fire had destroyed the greater part.

As it was no longer a Basset family home, maybe the family felt that its grand porch and other ornamentation should be removed to decorate properties that were. Perhaps Pilton House, near Barnstaple[169], benefitted, but the porch was re-erected and is still at Westaway, which was another Basset home, also on the outskirts of Barnstaple.

The 'elaborate carved work' went to Watermouth Castle. Its development had 'begun in 1825, but c. 1845 (had been) taken in hand, a mere shell...for Arthur [Davie] Basset.' As its 'builder', his embellishments included the initials of his wife, Harriet Sarah, née Crawforth, above the Castle's clock-tower door.

Between the 'begun' and 'taken in hand' dates, Victoria had become Queen, so, although it may appear older, the Castle that overlooks Watermouth Cove is mainly a Victorian structure. Its chronicles are erratic, but it is known that a building has been here for centuries.

An 'ancient map' includes the shape of a cross,

---

169 This is about half-a-mile north of the town. It is a spacious and impressive-looking Georgian mansion, which had been a family home to the Incledons, the Chichesters and the Bassets before it was purchased in 1948 to become a care home for the elderly.

APPENDICES

which is the site of 'an old foundation... in the tunnels.' It has been suggested that this was the location for a monastery, but, additionally, there is belief that there may have been 'a small fort...to defend the cove against privateers.'[170]

Other ancient remains exist behind the Castle and there are visible foundations in its dungeons. No date has been scratched into this stone work; however, it is known that they pre-date the structure that we can see today.

Additionally, there is printed evidence to prove that there was *something* at Watermouth long before the Basset family inherited because Nicholas Wichehalse purchased a '16th Century Manor of Watermouth' and a baptismal register from St Peter's church, Berrynarbor, includes another verification, as an Elizabethan entry, of '1566' mentions 'Elnor Taylor' whose birthplace was described as 'Watermouth'.

History continued to repeat itself during the Bassets' ownership: male family members accepted surname change. Arthur and Harriet's son, Arthur Crawforth Davie Basset, died childless, 'without issue'. Ownership continued through the female line; his sister, the eldest daughter, Harriet Mary, who had married Charles Henry Williams in 1858, inherited. Like Joseph Davie before him, Charles Henry Williams 'assumed the name of Basset' on the death of a relative, because, on this occasion, it complied with his brother-in-law's will.

Charles and Harriet Williams had a daughter then a son. Edith was born in Umberleigh and baptised at Atherington on the 14th July 1861. Her brother, Walter was born in September 1863 and baptised on the 7th November of the same year, also at Atherington.

She was baptised as 'Edith Basset Williams' because her birth had occurred before her father adopted 'Basset' as his surname by 'Royal Licence' in 1880.

Edith and Walter were the grand-children of Arthur Davie Basset: Watermouth's 'builder'.

Two large paintings hang in the Manor Hall: a landscape and a portrait. The latter is of Edith as a married woman. It is signed by 'A. Bright' and dated '1897'. She would have been about thirty-six when she had posed, perhaps in the grounds of her marital

Edith Penn Curzon.

Lieutenant Walter B. Basset, The Engineer.

---

170 Unfortunately, 'privateers' existed 'from ancient times until the 19th century', so this does not help to date this stone evidence.

Mrs Penn Curzon (seated), her nurses and patients, May 1916.

home, Pilton House, because she had married Major Ernest Charles Penn Curzon of the 18th and 3rd Hussars in 1882.

Edith and Walter's father died in 1908 and their mother died just before Ron's fourth birthday, in 1920:

'They were before my time mind. The owners I knew were Major and Mrs Penn Curzon. *They* were the *celebrities* of our day. The Penn Curzon's did mix; you didn't see a lot of them, but they came to concerts now and again.

It was always the villagers that worked for them. They had a chauffeur, Walter Snell; he would drive them around. He lived in a cottage in the castle grounds. They had gardeners too. My stepfather Jack worked there for a while; Alfie Leworthy and Alf Brooks did too, but Alf did carpentry for them as well, when he couldn't go outside. They had about six greenhouses and they had cold frames. My granny, Ellen Toms, she worked for them and my Aunt Lizzie did too.

The path by the bridge, at the top of Haggington Hill, takes you down to the Castle. The road was a good solid road, not Tarmacked though, but it was looked after. If the gardeners saw it looking bad, perhaps after heavy rain, they'd borrow the steam roller from the council and make it better. If they saw anything breaking up, they'd roller it down.'

A small fragile booklet, 'Mrs Penn Curzon's Hospital for Officers, September 27th 1919', shows that 'Promptly after the outbreak of the Great War, Major and Mrs Penn Curzon offered the use of Watermouth Cottage as a residence for convalescing wounded soldiers, and as promptly was it taken advantage of.'

In 1918, Edith received a CBE for this work because she and her mother, Mrs Harriet Basset, are recorded as 'working tirelessly' to provide a 'Convalescent Home for Wounded British and Belgian soldiers, 1914-15' (and) afterwards a Convalescent Home for Officers until the end of the Great War.' During this time, they looked after over 600 men.

Walter had died before their father, in 1907, but furthermore, he too had been childless. Once their parents were deceased, the female line inherited yet again. Their only daughter, Edith Penn Curzon, became the Castle's owner. Initially, this impressive building suffered, as by 1923 White's had to describe it as 'now unoccupied... an embattled mansion of stone'.

Ron had commented:

'The Watermouth Castle painting in the Manor Hall was big enough to almost cover the front of the stage. It was on a roller blind and you'd pull it up. There was space for the stairs either side.'

This landscape painting of the Castle is a likeness of what can be seen today.

◇ APPENDICES ◇

Watermouth Castle, 2012.

From an original watercolour drawing, 'Bullocks near Watermouth Castle'.

Edith Penn Curzon was widowed in 1938, but Ron can remember the Major:

'Charlie Ley worked as a gardener for Major Penn Curzon on the estate. It looked the same as today, but there weren't any visitors. It had a big garden that employed about eight men; the beach and towards the lookout was theirs too.

'The Warren' was the lookout area. I cleared the footpaths here with a hook. Bob Richards was my Boss then; Fred had died. The Watermouth Cove footpath has been in public use for years. Major Penn Curzon didn't like it if he saw us. He used to fire a gun, not at us, but to scare us away. He used binoculars to look out and if we didn't move he'd send a dog. The lookout was nicknamed the pigeon house. We used to walk to here regularly; courting couples used it on Sunday afternoons and light evenings. We went by the boathouse and on to the path. It was just fields and grasslands before the caravan site, which were rented by Lydford Farm; Mr Bert Watts had bullocks here.'

Edith returned to the family's Scottish estate in 1942, but her life ended in 1943, the same year that Ron had begun a new chapter of his life as a married man. Her tombstone is in Berrynarbor churchyard. Edith died on 30 April and was 81 at the time of her registered death.

In 1946, the last Basset to live at Watermouth, Edith's only daughter, Lorna, Countess of Howe, left the castle, perhaps also for their Scottish home. In the same year, a September issue of the *North Devon Journal* disclosed that her brother, Charles Ernest Bassett Lothian Curzon, had instructed that the castle be 'sold privately... for use as an hotel.'

It lay empty for a few years and ownership change continued, but it did not become a hotel. It was opened to the public in 1949 and, later, was offered to the National Trust, but this was declined.

Later another owner wished to convert it all to luxury flats and yet another opened the castle as a museum.

For about twelve years it was empty again until the current owners bought a near-derelict property in 1977. After another major restoration project, its 'ground floor and dungeons' are now home to one of North Devon's 'premier tourist attractions'.

Bibliography

A.J.A. Blake, (1995), *Berrynarbor A Short History*. Ilfracombe: Kingsley.

Beagley, D. *St Peter's Church Berrynarbor.*

Beaumont, G.F. (1996), *The Story of Combe Martin*. 9th ed. Ilfracombe: North Devon Print.

Bovett, R. (1989), *Historical Notes on Devon Schools*. Devon County Council.

B.T. The Phone Book. Devon North 2010/11.

Butterfield J, (Ed) (2003), *Collins English Dictionary*. 6th ed. Glasgow: HarperCollins.

Cherry, B. & Pevsner, N. (1989), *The Buildings of England*. London: Penguin.

Downes, J. (1998), *A Guide to Devon Dialect*. 2nd ed. Padstow: Tabbhouse.

Evans, I. H. (1989), *Brewer's Dictionary of Phrase & Fable*. 14th ed. London: Guild.

Vernon C. (June 2010), *Focus Magazine*. Ilfracombe: Kingsley.

Hanks, P. & Hodges, F. (1999), *A Dictionary of Surnames*. Oxford: O.U.P.

Hawkins, M. (1988), *Devon Roads*. Exeter: Wheaton Publishers Ltd.

Gover, J.E.B, Mayer, A. and Stenton, F.M. (1969) *The Place-Names of Devon*.Part 1. Cambridge: University Press.

(1936), *Ilfracombe and North Devon Directory and Year Book*. Ilfracombe: *Ilfracombe Chronical & North Devon News.*

(1933), *Kelly's Directory of Barnstaple and District.*

(1935), *Kelly's Directory of Devon.*

Marten, C. (1992), *The Devonshire Dialect*. Newton Abbot: Peninsula Press.

Mills, A.D. (1998), *Oxford Dictionary of British Place Names*. Oxford: OUP.

Palmer, M.G. *Watermouth Castle*. Ilfracombe. The Chronicle Press Ltd.

Parkhouse, Neil. (2001), *A glance back at... Lydney Docks*. Lydney: Black Dwarf Publications.

Penn Curzon E. (1919), *Mrs Penn Curzon's Hospital for Officers*. Watermouth Castle.

Pullen S. and Harding J. (2003), *Images of England - Ilfracombe*. Stroud: Tempus Publishing Ltd.

Raban, S. (1999), *The Countryman*. Skipton: The Country Publications Ltd.

Sellman, R.R. (1984), *Early Devon Schools*. Devon County Council.

St Peter's Church, Berrynarbor. Leaflet

Upshall, M. (1992), *The Hutchinson Pocket Encyclopaedia*. Oxford: Helicon Publishing.

(1895) *The Visitations of the County of Devon comprising the Heralds' Visitations of 1531, 1564 & 1620, with additions by Lt. Col. J.L. Vivian*. Henry S. Eland.

Wall, R. (1973), *Bristol Channel Pleasure Steamers*. Newton Abbott: David & Charles.

Watermills in North Devon Group, *Watermills in North Devon* 1994, Ilfracombe: Kingsley.

Watkins, D. (1995), *RAF Chivenor*. Stroud: Alan Sutton Publishing Ltd.

Yates, B. (1998) *North Devon Coast in Old Photographs*. Rochester: Universal Books Ltd

www.archive.timesonline.co.uk

www.barnstaplepanniermarket.co.uk

www.bbc.co.uk/weather

www.britishistoryonline

www.churchsociety.org

www.devonandcornwallwools.co.uk

www.devonclosewool.co.uk

www.devon.gov.uk

www.direct.gov.uk

www.disused-stations.org.uk

www.exmoor-nationalpark.gov.uk

www.farm-direct.co.uk

www.history.petop.co.uk

www.historyof central heating...

www.ironbridge.org.uk

www.listedbuildings.co.uk

www.merl.co.uk

www.middle-ages.org.uk

www.midwestdistancedriving.org/harness-parts

www.modbs.co.uk

www.northdevon.gov.uk

www.piltonhouse.co.uk

www.ploughmen.co.uk

www.redrubydevon.co.uk

www.simetric.co.uk

www.ukagriculture.com

www.vintageadvertisingprints.co.uk

www.william1.co.uk

www.whott.co.uk

Subscribers

Paul C. E. Adam, Horsham, West Sussex
Katrina L. Adam, Otley, Yorkshire
Freya E. L. Adam, Horsham
Mark and Hilary Adams, Capel Cottage
Janice Alcock, The Woodlands House, Sterridge Valley, Berrynarbor
Mr M. And Mrs W. Amos-Yeo, The Old Rectory, Berrynarbor
Mrs C. Anderson, Baughurst, Hampshire
Colin and Wendy Applegate, Berrynarbor
Gemma Bacon, Monks Path, Barton Lane, Berrynarbor
Tom Bartlett, Tower Cottage, Berrynarbor
Inge Bartlett, Tower Cottage, Berrynarbor
Jill and Barry Bentley, relatives of Ron Toms
For the Children of Berrynarbor
Sheila (daughter of Ron Toms) and Tony Bolt, Swindon
Craig Bolt (Grandson of Ron Toms) and family, Swindon
Darren Bolt (Grandson of Ron Toms) and family, Swindon
Patrick W. L. Bonds
Valerie Noreen Bowden
John and Fenella Boxall, Berrynarbor
Silas E. J. Brookman Braund, Goosewell
Phil and Chris Brown, Middle Lee Farm, Berrynarbor, Devon
K. J. Burrow, Bucks Cross, Devon
Camplin, Tidbury and Burgess, Barton Lane
Chris and Jen Caswell, Berrynarbor Park
Sally Cave-Browne-Cave, London (distant relative of Ron Toms)
In memory of the Challacombes of Haggington Hill
Mike Cottee (formerly of Combe Martin)
Jeff and Angela Davis, St Austell
Gladys and Ron Dyer
Barbara and Alan Eales, Barton Hill, Berrynarbor
Robert and Carol Flynn, Laleham

Felicity Francis, Holmbury St Mary
Miss Charlotte Fryer and Mr Michael Davison, The Village, Silver Street, Berrynarbor
Chris and Barbara Gubb
Robin Harding, Combe Martin
Sue and Jeremy Hill, Devon Cottage, Berrynarbor
Mr F. E. Hillier
Bob and Eileen Hobson, Berrynarbor
Bill Huxtable, Berrynarbor
Susan Huxtable-Selly, formerly of Combe Martin
Chris and Wendy Jenner, Berrynarbor
Sue Jones, Whitley Cottage, Berrynarbor, Devon
Brian Jones, Berrynarbor Park, Berrynarbor
Barbara Jordan, Weymouth
Isabella Kennedy, Berrynarbor, Devon
Tony Kitchin, Berrynarbor
Josephine M. Lane, Brookside, 63 The Village, Berrynarbor
Laura J. Lethaby, Birdswell Lane, Berrynarbor, Devon
Vera Lewis (née Ley), ex Orchard House
William H. Leworthy, Manor House
Tanya Lihou (née Walls), St Peter Port, Guernsey
Sue Longbottom, Australia
Gillian Loosemore, Brookmead, Berrynarbor, Devon
June and Gerry Marangone
Mr P. J. Moyle, Cove, Farnborough, Hants
Elaine Northey, Ystradgynlais, Swansea
Gill and Andy O'Reilly, Langleigh Guest House
Karen, Callum, Morgan and Roker Ozelton, Ye Olde Globe, Berrynarbor
Jean and Peter Pell, Sterridge Valley, Berrynarbor
Louise Powers (née Walls), Anna Bay, NSW 2316, Australia
Frederick E. Redmore, Ilfracombe, Devon
Kate Rees and Seretse Williams, Berrynarbor
Andrew Reeve (Son of Noel Reeve), Farnborough, Hampshire
Michael Richards, Napps, Old Coast Road, Berrynarbor

Marilyn Richards, Nethercombe, West Challacombe Lane, Combe Martin, Devon
Randall Richards, Bystock Court, Exmouth, Devon
Mrs Ingeburg Richardson, Sherrards, Barton Lane, Berrynarbor
Bruce and Sheila Roberts, Great Bookham, Surrey
Alan and Nora Rowlands, Briar Cottage, Berrynarbor
Jeanne Rumson-Waltho, Church Street, Combe Martin
Flora B. E. Segbefia Braund, Goosewell
Jill Sidebottom, Grandaughter of Fred Richards
Mrs J. D. Songhurst
Mrs S. Stratton, Crawley, West Sussex
Mr Ephraim Street, Rose Cottage
Mrs Grace Timms, Highways, Barton Lane, Berrynarbor

Wilfred and Valerie Toms
Mary Tucker, Copper Beech, Sterridge Valley, Berrynarbor
Mrs Eve Walker, Berrynarbor
Matthew Walls, Berrynarbor
Mrs H. Watkins, Combe Martin, Devon
Mike and Ann Williams, Sterridge Valley, Berrynarbor
Nick and Zoe Williams, Devon Cottage, Berrynarbor
Pamela Wilton (née Newton), Woodlands, Combe Martin, Devon
Mr Paul Spencer Wood, Orchard House, Berrynarbor, Devon
R. Wright, Charlotte Avenue, Wickford, Essex
E. P. Wright (née Draper), Regents Court, Pownall Road, Hackney, London